JEAN JACQUES BURLAMAQUI

From an oil painting by R. Gardelle

Jean Jacques Burlamaqui

A LIBERAL TRADITION

IN AMERICAN CONSTITUTIONALISM

By

RAY FORREST HARVEY, PH. D.

Department of Government
Washington Square College
New York University

*

Chapel Hill

THE UNIVERSITY OF NORTH CAROLINA PRESS

1937

A contribution from the American Council of Learned
Societies has assisted in the publication of this volume.

TO EDRENA

PREFACE

JEAN JACQUES BURLAMAQUI as a source of American
constitutionalism has never before been treated. Yet, he is,
demonstrably, a primary source of the theory voiced in
the Declaration of Independence. Moreover, the principles
of his constitutional system are strikingly like those of the
American.

Indeed, there is a Burlamaquian tradition running
through American political theory. This has been both a
conscious and an unconscious tradition. The publication of
his work at the middle of the eighteenth century was
timely from the American point of view. Also, it was a
philosophy of the new politics; a philosophy of the rising
middle class. It was not, however, an extremely pragmatic
philosophy in that it did not accept or propagate all the
principles of the theory of a business civilization. It was a
progressive theory containing the vitalizing principle of
social justice as its core. Its emergence in American political thinking has been always at the hands of the more
socially minded leaders, such as Jefferson, Wilson, and
Franklin D. Roosevelt.

For aid in the preparation of this work I wish to acknowledge the assistance of the Librarians, too numerous
to mention by name, who gave of their time in answering
inquiries and ferreting out material. Especially do I wish

to express my thanks to Professors R. J. Swenson and Clyde Eagleton of New York University, B. R. Wright, Jr. of Harvard, and Cortez A. M. Ewing of the University of Oklahoma, who have read all or parts of the manuscript. I wish to thank Professor Chinard of the University of California for his unceasing interest in the preparation of this work. To Professor Charles Coleman Thach of New York University, under whose direction I originally began this study, I owe a debt of gratitude for his untiring efforts and assistance and his sympathetic counsel. Always he was more than willing to give of his time and energy to the successful completion of the work. To him, here, I can only express my thanks. To the American Council of Learned Societies I am indebted for material aid in its publication.

To Edrena Fincher Harvey I acknowledge my indebtedness for her patient and sympathetic understanding during the writing of the manuscript. Naturally, I assume all responsibility for any errors of judgment or fact in the book.

RAY F. HARVEY

New York City
May 20, 1937

CONTENTS

PART I

THE POLITICAL PHILOSOPHY
OF
JEAN JACQUES BURLAMAQUI

1

THE NATURE OF THE STATE

WHILE WE have paid homage to certain political philosophers as marking the beginning of this or that idea, or as marking the end of one era and the birth of a new; while we have been told specifically that the beginning of modern political theory was marked by the return to the precepts of the Greeks by Montesquieu and Rousseau, no attempt has been made to evaluate the political philosophy of the Swiss jurist, Jean Jacques Burlamaqui, or to find his place in the development of modern political thought. And yet it may be demonstrated that Burlamaqui made definite advances beyond his predecessors and unique contributions in the field of political philosophy.

To the American student, particularly, these advances are of special interest, for they lead Burlamaqui to conclusions of the greatest significance to constitutional theory. If the most essential principles of our constitutionalism can not be logically derived from Locke's teachings and only to a small degree from Montesquieu, and if, on the other hand, these principles, in what is normally regarded as the peculiarly American form, are found elaborated in Burlamaqui's work, a presumption is established that the theoretical discussion of the latter influenced the development of the practical political doctrine. This presumption ripens into a certainty in the light of the evidence presented in Part II of the present study.

It is intended, then, first to analyze the political philosophy of Burlamaqui with a view to demonstrating that it represents in fundamental respects advances over that of the preceding contractualists as, indeed, it differs from Rousseau's theories as developed in the subsequent *Social Contract*. This will be undertaken not only because the importance of these unique features fully warrants their independent study but because on this basis Burlamaqui developed a theory of constitutional government, unique in its day, strikingly like our own, and widely known in influential quarters at the very time when the American doctrine was being evolved.

To demonstrate fully the unique position of Burlamaqui, it is necessary to review briefly the antecedent concepts of the state. Especially is it essential that his teachings in this respect be contrasted with those of the social contract school, particularly of Hobbes, Locke and Rousseau. By this method only is it possible to assign to him his place in the field of political thought.

It is the purpose of this chapter to show that, although accepting many of the principles of the contractualists, he departed decidedly from the teachings of that school. While using the phrases and terms common to his age, Burlamaqui was able to rise above it. While paying lip-service to certain contractualist doctrines, he revolted against the conventional or artificial nature of state and government—the cardinal principle of that school. Consciously he aimed at a restoration of political thinking to a more tenable basis. He attacked the concept of the state which presupposed an antagonism between the individual and political authority. Burlamaqui reintroduced into political thinking the concepts of Plato and Aristotle.

1

According to the Greek political theorists, notably Plato and Aristotle, the state was an institution natural to man. The state, they contended, did not come into existence as a result of a definite and positive act. No distinction was made between natural man and political man. The state was an inevitable and natural evolution. This concept eliminated from their thinking the necessity for an ethical justification of an artificial or conventional state which sprang full-grown from the brain of man. The Greeks, particularly Aristotle, contended therefore that political coercion needed no other justification than natural coercion. In the words of Aristotle: "When several villages are united in a single complete community, large enough to be nearly or quite self-sufficing, the state comes into existence, originating in the bare needs of life, and continuing in existence for the sake of a good life. And therefore, if the earlier forms of society are natural, so is the state, for it is the end of them, and the nature of a thing is its end. For what each thing is when fully developed, we call its nature, whether we are speaking of a man, a horse, or a family. Besides, the final cause and end of a thing is the best, and to be self-sufficing is the end and the best. Hence it is evident that the state is a creation of nature, and that man is by nature a political animal."[1] This concept of the

[1] Aristotle, *Works* (B. Jowett, tr. Oxford, Clarendon Press, 1921), Vol. X, Bk. I, Ch. II, par. 1252b.

origin of the state prevailed until the Stoics cast it aside in
favor of the "convention" theory as not constituting a true
basis for its existence.

The concept of the origin of the state held by the mediaevalists, to which the contractualists paid unfaltering
homage, was a direct antithesis of the Aristotelian idea. It
was held to be founded upon convention. That is, to the
mediaeval philosophers the state was a man-made institution which had no essential relation to the natural and
original character of man. Civil society was an artificial
something superimposed on man by man himself. It
could not be justified on the basis of his true nature. Its
whole existence must rest upon a convention necessitated
by his degeneration from his original perfection, its purpose being the negative one of restraint of sin. Beginning
with the Stoics, though it was not unknown in Plato's day,
this idea remained the dominant characteristic of political
philosophy until the middle of the eighteenth century.

This mediaeval concept formed the keystone of the
social contract school of thought. Hooker, Grotius, Hobbes,
Pufendorf, Locke and Rousseau, representative of the
growth of this concept in the sixteenth, seventeenth and
eighteenth centuries, clung tenaciously to the idea that
man originally was in a pre-political state of nature and
that he must transfer himself by an overt act from the
natural into the civil state.

The fundamental premise or common point of departure of the contractualists was the state of nature. In unison they declared man to be equal in nature, a conclusion
basic to their concept of consent as the theoretical basis of
state and government. In the interpretation of the state of
nature, they were divided into two groups; of the one

Hobbes and Rousseau[2] are representative, while to the other belong Locke and Burlamaqui. In the end each justified, in his own way, by some form of consent, the right of the state to be and its right to continue to exist.

To Hobbes the state of nature was one of perpetual warfare. Every man was at war with every other man. Natural man was a thoroughly anti-social and non-moral being. As a materialist Hobbes saw all of man's actions determined by the impulse of self-preservation. Self-preservation manifested itself through two all-absorbing forces: fear on the one hand and desire for power on the other. Fear of retribution was the only restraint preventing the commission of anti-social acts. A desire for power, not merely for immediate purposes but to guarantee a continuing satisfaction of his needs, was the dominating faculty of the Hobbesian man. He had no sense of justice. The ideas of just and unjust were adjuncts of political society only.[3]

"I put for a general inclination of all mankind," Hobbes wrote, "a perpetual and relentless desire of power after power that ceaseth only in death. And the cause of this is not always that a man hopes for a more intensive delight than he has already attained to, or that he cannot be content with a more moderate power; but because he cannot

[2] Rousseau's being bracketed with Hobbes may, at first sight, seem peculiar in view of his frequent idealization of natural man. See *infra*, p. 7.

[3] Thomas Hobbes, *Leviathan* (Everyman Edition, New York, E. P. Dutton & Company, 1928), Pt. I, Ch. XIII, p. 66. "To this warre of every man against every man, this also is consequent, that nothing can be unjust. The notions of Right and Wrong, Justice and Injustice have there no place. Where there is no common power, there is no law; where there is no law, no Injustice. Force and Fraud are in warre the two Cardinall virtues. Justice and Injustice are not of the Faculties neither of the body or mind. They are qualities that relate to men in society, not in Solitude."

assure the power and means to live well, which he hath at present, without the acquisition of more."[4]

Man, however, was naturally a rational being. By granting to him this faculty, Hobbes established a basis upon which man could bring himself out of the state of nature and into civil society. With the other contractualists, Hobbes recognized the utilitarian purpose of the state. Natural man would want to give up his natural state in return for civil society if by so doing he could gain peace and security. This constituted the appeal of political authority as the common judge over all.

By ascribing anti-social faculties to man, Hobbes closed the door on any possibility of constructing a state on grounds other than the mediaeval idea of its un-naturalness. The state and man were to be antagonistic in their relationship except as the state could fulfill the purposes of its inception. The legal and ethical justification for the exercise of political authority was based upon the contract which had brought the state into being. In direct reference to Aristotle's statement concerning bees and ants, Hobbes repudiated the Aristotelian idea. "The agreement of these creatures is Naturall," he wrote, "that of man is of Covenant only, which is artificial."[5]

Rousseau's pre-social man does not differ essentially from that described by Hobbes. It has been pointed out by an eminent scholar, Professor A. O. Lovejoy, that Rousseau divided pre-political society into four states.[6] In the last period Rousseau described man as being similar in characteristics and nature to the Hobbesian man. It was a

[4] *Ibid.*, Ch. XII, p. 49.

[5] *Ibid.*, Pt. II, Ch. XVII, p. 89.

[6] A. O. Lovejoy, "The Supposed Primitivism of Rousseau's Discourse on Inequality," *Modern Philology*, XXI (November, 1923), 165-86. Cited by W. W. Willoughby, *The Ethical Basis of Political Authority*, pp. 199-204.

state marked by licentiousness, by perpetual war. It would appear, however, that in the following passage Rousseau granted man a certain moral understanding. "Contemplating the first and most simple operations of the human soul, I think that I can perceive two principles prior to reason, one of them deeply interesting us in our own welfare and preservation, and the other exciting a natural repugnance at seeing our species suffer pain and death. It is from the agreement and combination which the understanding is in a position to establish between these two principles, without its being necessary to introduce that of sociability, that all the rules of natural right appear to me to be derived—rules which our reason is afterwards obliged to establish on other foundations when by its successive developments it has been led to suppress nature itself." [7]

But, although here vaguely admitting an innate feeling of sympathy in man, Rousseau in the *Social Contract* definitely aligned himself with Hobbes as the following statement demonstrates: "The passage from the state of nature to the civil state produces in man a very remarkable change, by substituting in his conduct justice for instinct, and by giving his actions the moral quality they had previously lacked." [8]

In the words of a modern commentator: "The passage from the state of nature to the civil state" resulted in the individual's exchanging natural liberty "for a liberty at

[7] In his Preface to *A Discourse on Inequality*, quoted in Willoughby, *op. cit.*, p. 201.

[8] J. J. Rousseau, *Social Contract* (Everyman Edition, New York, E. P. Dutton & Company, 1923), Bk. I, Ch. VIII, p. 18. Continuing further: "What man loses by the social contract is his natural liberty and an unlimited right to anything which tempts him and which he is able to attain; what he gains is civil liberty and property in all that he possesses." Cf. Lovejoy, *op. cit.*

once limited and secured by the general will. He exchanges the mere possession of such things that he can get, a possession which is the effect of force, for a property founded on a positive title, on the guarantee of society. At the same time he becomes a moral agent. Now for the first time it can be said that there is any thing which he *ought* to do, as distinguished from that which he is *forced* to do."[9]

It is not maintained that Rousseau belongs to the mediaeval period of philosophy. Most of his thinking is far from it. But he did have, in common with Hobbes, Locke and the mediaevalists, the concept which should not be ignored that changes were effected in man because of the social contract. He could not rid himself of the idea that political power was not natural. Of necessity the state was an artificial development.

Locke, in contrast to Hobbes and Rousseau, viewed man in the state of nature as a social being and obligated by the laws of nature. He was a social being because "God, having made such a creature that, in his own judgment, it was not good for him to be alone, put him under strong obligation of necessity, convenience, and inclination, to drive him into society, as well as fitted him with understanding and language to continue and enjoy it."[10] By nature social man would be motivated always by self-interest which would be tempered by community interests. Recognizing the presence of the law of nature, Locke's pre-political man had a yardstick by which he might judge right from wrong. On this basis he described the state of natural man as "a state of perfect freedom to order their actions, and dispose of their possessions and persons as they think fit,

[9] T. H. Green, *Lectures on the Principles of Political Obligation*, pp. 81-82.
[10] John Locke, *Of Civil Government* (Everyman Edition, New York, E. P. Dutton and Company, 1924), Bk. II, Ch. VII, par. 77, pp. 154-55.

within the bounds of the law of nature, without asking leave or depending upon the will of any other man."[11] Locke was quick to point out that although liberty existed, yet it was not a state of license. In contrast with Hobbes' state of nature, that of Locke was better ordered and a more desirable place in which to live.

Although describing pre-political man as naturally social, Locke failed to take advantage of the opening presented to found the state upon the broad concept of its naturalness to man. Consequently, the characteristically mediaeval principle of convention was as thoroughly a part of Locke's theoretical discussion of the state as it was of Hobbes. In many respects he was more emphatic in his denial of its naturalness. Regarding the state of nature, he wrote: "But I, moreover, affirm that all men are naturally in that state, and remain so till, by their own consents, they make themselves members of some politic society, and I doubt not, in the sequel of this discourse, to make it very clear."[12] Man can bring himself out of the state of nature only by his own act. Moreover, Locke insisted that this could be done only through a particular kind of compact. "For it is not every compact that puts an end to the state of nature between men, but only this one of agreeing together mutually to enter into one community, and make one body politic; other promises and compacts man may make one with another, and yet still be in the state of nature."[13] Political or civil society is instituted "wherever any number of men, in the state of nature, enter into society to make one people one body politic under one supreme government. And this puts men out of a state of

11 *Ibid.*, Ch. II, par. 4, p. 118.
12 *Ibid.*, par. 15, p. 124.
13 *Ibid.*, par. 14, p. 124.

nature into that of a commonwealth. . . . And wherever there are any number of men, however associated, that have no such decisive power to appeal to, there they are still in the state of nature."[14]

Relative to the Aristotelian and the mediaeval theories of the origin of the state, the Carlyles may be cited as representative of the commentators upon the date of the beginning of modern theory. "The political theory of the Middle Ages," they write, "is formally separated from that of Aristotle and Plato, and from that of the nineteenth century, by one great presupposition—that is, that the institutions of civilized society are founded upon 'convention', not upon 'nature'. Not, indeed, that this distinction is only mediaeval, for it continued to dominate European thought until the latter part of the eighteenth century. It is, indeed, only with Montesquieu, Rousseau's 'Contrat Social', and Burke that the characteristically modern return to the Aristotelian and Platonic mode was established."[15]

This quotation is not incorrect. Rather it is incomplete in that it fails to take into account the work of Burlamaqui. The Aristotelian idea was accepted by Burlamaqui in his *Principes du droit naturel,* 1747, in a conscious effort to reinstate it as the paramount concept of the basis of the state. He justified his detailed "reflections" on the nature and faculties of pre-political man because "they are extremely proper for removing the false notions which most people have upon this subject; as if the civil state could not be established but in prejudice to their liberty, and as if the government had been invented only to satisfy the am-

[14] *Ibid.,* Ch. VII, par. 89, p. 160.

[15] R. W. and A. J. Carlyle, *A History of Mediaeval Political Theory in the West,* V, 4.

bition of designing men contrary to the interest of the rest
of the community.''[16]

2

Burlamaqui was not, then, a proponent of the contractualist dogma that the state was an artificial institution superimposed upon man to restrain and curb his
natural liberty. The individual, to him, could not be actually or potentially at war with political power—the
belief presupposed and fostered by the convention theory
of the origin of the state. The latter was the prevailing
theory and the one that he set out to destroy. For the convention theory he substituted the theory in which the state
was the natural and necessary result of the evolution of
man. On the basis of a sociological interpretation Burlamaqui concluded that man and political power are not
antithetical. He postulated a positive as opposed to a negative theory of the state.

Burlamaqui was more emphatic than any philosopher
after Aristotle in his belief that man was essentially a social
creature. "They [men] are all inhabitants of the same
globe, placed in a kind of vicinity to each other; have all
one common nature, the same faculties, same inclinations,
wants and desires." Advancing the idea that man had no
choice in the matter, "I am not the only person upon
earth," he wrote, "I find myself in the middle of an infinite number of men, who resemble me in every respect;
and I am subject to this state even by my nativity itself,

[16] J. J. Burlamaqui, *Principles of Natural and Politic Law*, 2 vols. (3rd ed.,
Thomas Nugent, tr. London, C. Nourse, 1784), Vol. II, Pt. I, Ch. III, par.
xxviii, p. 20. (Volume II of this edition is cited throughout as *Politic Law*,
unless a notation to the contrary is made.)

by the very act of providence.''[17] But the social nature of man goes far deeper than mere geographical proximity. His physical, mental and spiritual make-up are not in and of themselves an end. Taken alone they are incapable of attaining the satisfaction of a well-rounded whole. This fuller life for which man strives requires and demands the presence of and assistance of other men. It does not follow, however, that man loses his individuality in this process. Like Plato and Aristotle, Burlamaqui observed that "nature has thought proper to distribute differently her talents among men, by giving some an aptitude to perform certain things well. . . . Wherefore if the natural wants of men render them dependent on one another the diversity of talents, which qualifies them for mutual succor, connects and unites them."[18]

The nature of man is such that he has no desire to avoid society. He is repelled by the thought of being alone because it is not satisfying. Solitude makes no appeal for "our hearts are naturally bent to wish for the company of our equals, and to dread an entire solitude as an irksome and forlorn state. Nothing is so satisfying and flattering to man as to think he merits the friendship and esteem of others."[19] War is not a state towards which man will be drawn; for, then, he could not satisfy his "wants and desires." The physical nature of man is constantly urging him to associate with his fellows. "Man," Burlamaqui wrote, "at all ages stands in need of several external succors for his nourishment. . . . For this reason our Creator

[17] J. J. Burlamaqui, *The Principles of Natural Law*, 2 vols. (2nd ed., Thomas Nugent, tr. London, J. Nourse, 1752), Vol. I, Pt. II, Ch. IV, par. lx, p. 163. (Volume I of this edition is cited throughout as *Natural Law* unless a notation to the contrary is made.)

[18] *Ibid.*, par. lxiii, p. 167.

[19] *Ibid.*, par. lxiv, p. 167.

has sown plentifully around us such things as are necessary for our wants, and he has implanted in us at some
time the instincts and qualifications proper for applying
these things to our advantage. The natural state, therefore, of man considered in this light, and in respect to the
goods of the earth, is a state of indigence and incessant
wants."[20]

Although recognizing the principle of economic de-
terminism, it did not lead him to the conclusion of the
contractualists that the state was an extraneous and foreign
element introduced into the life of man to deny him the
use of natural liberty. "Such, in effect, is the nature of
man that he necessarily loves himself, that he seeks in
every thing and every where his own advantage, and can
be never diverted from this pursuit."[21] Burlamaqui assumed a superior force which would at all times deter this
instinct of self-preservation and guide it in the direction
of the community good. "We naturally desire," he said,
"and necessarily wish for good. This desire anticipates all
our reflexions, and is not in our own election; it predomi-
nates in us, and becomes the *Primum mobile* of all our de-
terminations; our hearts being never inclined towards any
particular good, but by the natural impression which determines us to good in general. 'Tis not in our power to
change this bent of the will, which the Creator himself
has implanted in us." [22] This statement smacks of Rousseau's general will idea and of the whole eighteenth century democratic dogma. Rousseau was not unacquainted
with Burlamaqui. He mentions him by name in the Preface to *A Discourse on The Origin of Inequality*. Professor

[20] *Ibid.*, Pt. I, Ch. IV, par. v, p. 39.
[21] *Ibid.*, Ch. V, par. iv, p. 46.
[22] *Ibid.*

Charles Borgeaud demonstrates Rousseau's indebtedness to Burlamaqui.[23]

Society is natural to man for it is only in society that he is permitted to develop his many faculties. Only as he is free to use them to advantage is he approximating his ultimate purpose—happiness. Through society man has everything to gain and nothing to lose. Society is complementary to the individual. It does not destroy his individuality but in the broader sense permits him to attain that individuality, but within the greater whole, to its highest degree. Consequently, Burlamaqui views civil society as only "natural society itself, modified in such a manner, that there is a sovereign presiding over it, on whose will whatever relates to the welfare of the society ultimately depends; to the end that, by these means, mankind may attain, with greater certainty, that happiness to which they all naturally aspire." Logically, he concluded that only in society can "man find a remedy for the greatest part of his wants, and an occasion for exercising most of his faculties."[24]

The value of social institutions to Burlamaqui as to Aristotle rests upon their capacities to give reality to the faculties of will and reason; to be a positive force in the attainment of good. Thus the "adventitious" states, family, property and civil society, are only means to facilitate the realization of self-perfection in a social organization to which each contributes to the attainment of the good life of all. The civil state was to Burlamaqui the most important of all the "adventitious" states and it was instituted only to bring "men back to the observance of the laws of nature, and consequently to the road to happiness; it makes

---

[23] Charles Borgeaud, *Pages d'histoire nationale*, pp. 144 ff.
[24] *Politic Law*, Pt. I, Ch. I, par. iii, p. 2.

them return to their natural state, from whence they had strayed by the bad use which they made of their liberty."[25]

Burlamaqui attributed to man the faculties of knowing, perceiving, understanding, and acting. The power to will enabled man to rule out the undesirable and accept the desirable. The will "is nothing else," Burlamaqui wrote, "but the power of the soul, by which it is determined of itself, and by virtue of an active principle inherent in its nature, to seek for what is agreeable to it, to act after a certain manner, and to do or to omit an action, with a view to happiness."[26] The will must be free. Without liberty the power to will is impotent. Liberty to Burlamaqui was the power of making a choice, or "that force or power of the soul, whereby it modifies and regulates its operations as it pleases, so as to be able to suspend, continue, or alter its deliberations and actions; in a word, so as to be capable to determine and act with choice, according as it thinks proper."[27] He asked, "Can anyone seriously deny that in the choice of good and evil our resolves are unconstrained; that notwithstanding the first impressions, we have in our power to stop of a sudden, to weigh the arguments on both sides, and to do, in short, whatever can be expected from the freest agent? . . . I find I can abstain from it; I can hesitate in my choice; in short, I am my own master to chuse, or which is the same thing, I am free."[28]

Liberty does not imply license. Pre-political man had no right to do that which was contrary to the communal good.

[25] *Ibid.*, Ch. III, par. xxvii, p. 20. "Since civil liberty is far more preferable to that of nature, we may safely conclude, that the civil state, which procures this liberty to mankind, is of all human states the most perfect, the most reasonable, and of course the true natural state of man."

[26] *Natural Law*, Pt. I, Ch. II, par. i, p. 13.

[27] *Ibid.*, par. iii, p. 15.

[28] *Ibid.*, par. x, p. 24.

He was deterred from allowing his passions to run riot by
the restraining authority of the law of nature. His very
nature rebelled at license. "The laws of nature are," Burlamaqui said, "therefore the rule and measure of liberty;
and in the primitive and natural state, mankind have no
liberty but what the laws of nature give them; for which
reason it is proper to observe here, that the state of natural
liberty is not that of an entire independence."[29] In striking
contrast to the contractualists, and in agreement with
Aristotle, Burlamaqui made no essential distinction between natural and civil liberty. "Civil liberty," he concluded, "is natural liberty itself, divested of that part
which constituted the independence of individuals, by the
authority which it confers on sovereigns, and attended
with a right of insisting on his making a good use of his
authority, and with a moral security that this right will
have its effect."[30]

Upon this background Burlamaqui enunciated a startlingly new principle to modern political thought. One of
the inalienable rights of man, he declared, was happiness.
By this declaration the nature of the state was completely
transformed from its artificial basis as defended by the
contractualists to that of its naturalness. The justification
of the state was no longer to be found in its negative and
indirect aid to man. It became a constructive device committed to the task of not only permitting but actually taking the lead in securing for the individual this inalienable
right to happiness. The state assumed a positive responsibility to man. The purpose of man is the approximation to
happiness; the purpose of the state is to make for the fuller
life of the individual—happiness. This natural right is

[29] *Politic Law*, Pt. I, Ch. III, par. xvi, p. 16.
[30] *Natural Law*, Pt. I, Ch. IV, par. iii, p. 37.

universal in application. It has no hedonistic connotation. It is distinct from the utilitarian doctrine of happiness for the greatest number. Since the ultimate purpose of man and the state are identical and complementary there is no antagonism between the two. The justification of civil society lies in its naturalness to man. It needs no other explanation for the exercise of authority over the individual.

Burlamaqui states lucidly and concisely the thesis of his two-volume work in the first paragraph of the first chapter: "My design is to inquire into those rules which nature alone prescribes to man, in order to conduct him safely to the end, which every one has, and indeed ought to have, in view, namely, true and solid happiness. By *happiness* we are to understand the internal satisfaction of the soul, arising from the possession of good; and by good, whatever is suitable or agreeable to man for his preservation, perfection, conveniency, or pleasure. The idea of good determines that of evil, which in its most general signification, implies whatever is opposite to the preservation, perfection, conveniency, or pleasure of man."[31] Happiness is a natural and inalienable right of man. "The end of God in creating man was to render him happy. Upon this supposition it will be soon agreed that man cannot attain to happiness any other way than by the knowledge of truth and by the possession of real good."[32] Moreover, man is possessed of all the necessary faculties of attaining happiness. "Man is designed for happiness, and should certainly have been formed in such a manner as to find himself under an absolute necessity of desiring and pursuing good, and of shunning on the contrary evil in general."[33] All of the rights of

[31] *Ibid.*, Ch. II, par. i, p. 13.
[32] *Ibid.*, par. viii, p. 21.
[33] *Ibid.*, par. ix, pp. 22-23.

man are relative and only incidental to this greater and all-inclusive right. "Right ... is nothing else but whatever reason certainly acknowledges as a sure and concise means of attaining happiness, and approves as such."[34] Happiness is a natural and inalienable right because "the desire of happiness is as essential to man and as inseparable from his nature as reason itself."

Burlamaqui felt apologetic for the necessity of explaining this concept. "It may appear surprizing to some," he wrote, "that we should have stopped here, to investigate and explain the truth of a principle, which one would imagine is obvious to everybody, to the learned as well as the vulgar. And yet it was absolutely necessary; because this is a truth of the very last importance, which gives us the key, as it were, of the human system."[35] He complained that many "ethic writers" conceded happiness to be the end of man, but ignored it completely when they set up their systems of government.

3

As the contractualists were divided on the question of the sociability or non-sociability of pre-political man so, too, they were divided as to the character of natural law. Hobbes, conceiving an anti-social creature, denied the binding force of natural law. This position was necessary to his philosophy. On the other hand, Locke and Burlamaqui found it quite essential to their philosophy that natural law be a binding rule upon the actions of all men. However, in turn, these two differed in their interpreta-

[34] *Ibid.*, Ch. V, par. x, p. 51.
[35] *Ibid.*, par. vii, p. 48.

tion of the character of the law of nature. Locke analyzed it as a negative rule restraining man within that sphere of action absolutely essential to his well-being. It served as a policeman to prevent anti-social activities on the part of the members. To Burlamaqui it was a positive rule. It was more than a law simply protecting man from his fellows; it was a positive guide. By obeying its mandates one attained the ideal of the good life. As with the concept of the nature of the state, Burlamaqui expounds a broader philosophical basis of law than does Locke.[86]

The original connotation of "natural" in the phrase "natural right" was the opposite of "conventional." "Natural right is that which is right in and of itself apart from human institution."[87] It is more difficult to define the phrase "natural law." Law ordinarily implies a legislator. To the Greeks, nature was the legislator. The Stoics, believing in materialistic pantheism, held the true end and duty of man to be to live a life according to nature. Next, reason was introduced as a criterion of natural law. The legislator or giver of all law was "universal reason." As the centuries passed, this "universal reason" became too abstract, too far removed from the individual's power of conception and so disappeared. In its place arose the doctrine of the origin of natural law in right reason. According to Grotius, natural law is the "dictate of right reason, indicating that any act, from its agreement or disagreement with the rational nature, has in it moral turpitude or moral necessity."[88]

Burlamaqui was the last of the great natural law phi-

[86] For a more detailed discussion of this point see Chapter II.

[87] J. W. Salmond, "The Law of Nature," *Law Quarterly Review*, XI (April, 1895), 121.

[88] Hugo Grotius, *De Jure Belli ac Pacis* (W. Whewell, tr. Cambridge, 1853), Vol. I, Ch. I, par. 10, p. 1.

losophers. In the words of Professor Dickinson: "There
was little to be added to the formulation of the naturalist
dogma after Burlamaqui. . . . Perhaps the most exact and
systematic statement of the position of the naturalists was
that of Burlamaqui."[39] "Natural law," wrote Burlamaqui,
"is that which so necessarily agrees with the nature of and
state of man, that without observing its maxims neither
individuals, nor society can maintain themselves in an
honest and comportable state . . . the knowledge thereof
may be attained merely by the light of reason; and hence
is called natural."[40]

While admitting the restraining character of natural
law, which was secondary and incidental to its greater
purpose, he held it to be a body of guiding, positive principles. The state, argued Burlamaqui, was not a man-made
institution exercising a restraint on the use of natural
liberty by substituting civil liberty. No essential distinction, he contended, may be drawn between natural and
civil liberty. The laws of the state exist primarily as an aid
in the achieving of the end of man's existence—happiness.
The purpose of natural law, wrote Burlamaqui, "is not so
much to restrain the liberty of man as to make him act
agreeably to his real interests."[41] And "we should . . . take
care not to imagine that [civil] laws are properly made in
order to bring men under a yoke. . . . Let us say rather that
laws are made to oblige the subjects to act according to

[39] Edwin D. Dickinson, "Changing Concepts and the Doctrine of Incorporation," *American Journal of International Law*, XXVI (April, 1932), 247.

[40] *Natural Law*, Pt. I, Ch. X, par. 15, p. 110. Cf. Locke, *Of Civil Government*, Bk. II, Ch. II, par. 6, p. 119. "The state of nature has a law of nature
to govern it, which obliges every one, and reason, which is that law, teaches
all mankind who will but consult it, that being all equal and independent,
no one ought to harm another in his life, health, liberty, or possessions."

[41] *Politic Law*, Pt. I, Ch. III, par. xviii, p. 17.

their real interests, and to chuse the surest and best way to attain the end they are designed for, which is happiness."[42]

4

The contractualists were forced to assume a state of nature in which man was equal, rational, and possessed of reason in order to establish consent as the basis of the state. In regard to the state of nature and natural law they were divided into two groups; so it is with the social contract.

The paramount concept of Hobbes and Rousseau was essentially the same: the construction of an absolute state, the former with all power in one man, the latter, all power in the nation. Consequently, in agreement with their notions of the state of nature and of natural law, they, by one covenant, set up an artificial man and a real person, respectively, as the repository of all political power.

To Hobbes, man was impelled to seek to covenant with all others—to agree to forego the exercise of his power if each would consent to do the same—for a single, purely utilitarian and materialistic purpose. Civil society, the result of the contract, was instituted to replace the natural state, a concept strongly reminiscent of mediaeval notions.

"The only way to erect such a common power," wrote Hobbes, "as may be able to defend them from the invasion of foreigners, and the injuries of one another, and thereby to secure them in such sort, as that by their own industry, and by the fruits of the earth, they may nourish themselves and live contentedly, is to confer all their power and strength upon one man, or upon an assembly of men, that may reduce their will, by plurality of voices, into one will;

[42] *Natural Law*, Pt. I, Ch. X, par. iii, p. 99. Cf. Locke, *Of Civil Government*, Bk. II, Ch. VI, par. 57, p. 143.

which is as much as to say, to appoint one man, or assembly of men, to bear their person, and every man to own, and acknowledge himself to be author of whatsoever he that so beareth their person, shall act, or cause to be acted, in those things which concern the common peace and safety; and therein submit their wills, every one to his will, and their judgments, to his judgment. This is more than consent, or concord; it is a real unity of them all, in one and the same person, made by covenant of every man with every man, in such a manner, as if every man should say to every man 'I authorize and give up my right of governing myself, to this man, or to this assembly of men, on this condition, that thou give up thy right to him, and authorize all his actions in like manner.' This done, the multitude so united in one person is called a 'commonwealth', in Latin *civitas.*"[43]

By the social compact man had brought himself out of the state of nature. By the same act the "artificial man" was created. The latter possessed all power formerly belonging to each individual of the community. Also, the contract designated one man or an assembly of men as the medium through which the "artificial" man would speak. Because Hobbes recognized no rights anterior to the establishment of civil society he laid the foundation for an absolute state and government. This was a subversion of the normal doctrine which conceived political power as limited and justified revolution.[44]

Rousseau, in the following century, sought to create a real person by covenant. He, too, contended that the original compact transferred man from the state of nature into

---

[43] *Leviathan,* Pt. II, Ch. XVII, p. 89.

[44] *Ibid.,* Ch. XVIII, p. 90. "They that have already instituted a commonwealth, being thereby bound by covenant . . . cannot lawfully make a new covenant . . . without his permission."

civil society. The original compact was described by Rousseau as "the total alienation of each associate, together with all his rights, to the whole community; for, in the first place, as each gives himself absolutely, the conditions are the same for all; and, this being so, no one has any interest in making them burdensome to others. Moreover, the alienation being without reserve, the union is as perfect as it can be, and no associate has anything more to demand. ... At once, in place of the individual personality of each contracting party, this act of association creates a moral and collective body, composed of as many members as the assembly contains votes, and receiving from this act its unity, its common identity, its life and its will. This public person . . . is called by its members *State* when passive, *Sovereign* when active, and Power when compared with others like itself."[45] The element of absolutism, so characteristic of Hobbes, is, as it may be seen, present in Rousseau. But, it is the absolutism of the nation speaking through the "General Will."

Locke, a defender of the principles of limited state and government, found no reason for ascribing a fictitious or real personality to the state. Theoretically he had no intention of setting up a state which would be more powerful than the individuals which composed it. To do so would have denied his doctrine of the right of revolution which was founded upon natural and inalienable rights. The re-

[45] *Social Contract*, Bk. I, Ch. VI, pp. 15 ff. Perfect equality is guaranteed under this compact for "each man, in giving himself to all, gives himself to nobody; and as there is no associate over whom he does not acquire the same right as he yields others over himself, he gains an equivalent for everything he loses and an increase of force for the preservation of what he has. . . . Each of us puts his person and all of his power in common under the supreme direction of the general will, and, in our corporate capacity, we receive each member as an indivisible part of the whole."

sult of the social contract to Locke was a body politic having no overpowering personality. Of the original social compact Locke wrote: "When any number of men have so consented to make one community of government, they are thereby presently incorporated, and make one body politic, wherein the majority have a right to act and conclude the rest. For, when any number of men have, by the consent of every individual, made a community, they have thereby made that community one body, with a power to act as one body, which is only by the will and determination of the majority."[46] He avoids the full implication of this concept by maintaining the principle of popular sovereignty. In this light the body politic may be considered as so many people acting in unison rather than in the body politic as a nation. The law of nature remained constantly as a check upon the activities of the individual and consequently upon the state.

Burlamaqui, like Locke, enumerated inconveniences of the state of nature.[47] He observed, also, that "if mankind, during the time they lived in natural society, had exactly conformed to nature's laws, nothing would have been wanting to complete their happiness, nor would there have been any occasion to establish a supreme authority upon earth."[48] The problem faced by Burlamaqui was thus the same as that of all political philosophers. But he did not

[46] *Of Civil Government*, Bk. II, Ch. VIII, par. 96, p. 165. Certain inconveniences in the state of nature made the political state a necessity: (1) no "established, settled, known law"; (2) no "indifferent judge"; (3) often no "power to back and support the sentence when right, and to give it due execution." *Ibid.*, Ch. IX, pp. 179-81.

[47] *Politic Law*, Pt. I, Ch. III, pars. iv-viii, pp. 12-13. (1) "Passion soon weakened the force of nature's law"; (2) no common judge; (3) no one had the power to execute the law of nature.

[48] *Ibid.*, par. iii, p. 12.

answer it in the manner of his immediate predecessors. Instead, he returned to the basic precepts of Plato and Aristotle.

5

Manifestly Burlamaqui was not particularly concerned with the question of the historical origin of the state. "This is a question," he remarked, "rather curious than useful or necessary; the point of importance, and that particularly interesting to mankind, is to know whether the establishment of government, and of supreme authority, was really necessary, and whether mankind derive from thence any considerable advantages."[49] In conformity with his idea of the state of nature and of natural law, the justification of the state must be measured not by the means of its establishment but by the purpose which it serves.

In defining legitimate government he further shows his disregard for historical origins of state and government. "Governments of every kind, which are founded on the free acquiescence of the people, whether express or justified by a long and peaceable possession, are all equally legitimate, so long at least as, by the intention of the sovereign, they tend to promote the happiness of the people."[50] Emphatically, he wrote: "Nothing can be advanced with certainty concerning the real origin of civil societies. All that political writers say upon this subject is reduced to conjectures that have more or less probability."[51] Again, "the natural disposition of mankind, and their general manner of acting do not by any means permit us to refer

[49] *Ibid.*, Ch. II, par. viii, p. 11.
[50] *Ibid.*, Pt. II, Ch. II par. xiii, p. 87.
[51] *Ibid.*, Pt. I, Ch. II par. iii, p. 8.

the institution of all governments to a general and uniform principle." [52]

Nevertheless, after speaking of the contractual origin of the state, he observed that "though we are strangers to the original of most states, yet we must not imagine that what has been here said, concerning the manner in which civil societies are formed, is a mere fiction." [53] He accepted the contract as a plausible basis: "Since it is certain, that all civil societies had a beginning, it is impossible to conceive, how the members, of which they are composed, could agree to live together, dependent on a supreme authority, without supposing the covenants above-mentioned." [54] He observed that the founding of Rome might be an example of this type. [55]

On the basis of this discussion it appears quite convincingly that Burlamaqui did not accept the contentions of the contractualists in their entirety. He accepted the contractualist idea of covenant only as a probable and practical means of the origin of the state. As he modified their teachings with respect to the state of nature and natural

[52] *Ibid.*, par. vii, p. 9.

[53] *Ibid.*, Ch. IV, par. xvii, p. 29.

[54] *Ibid.*, par. xvi, p. 28. Cf. Locke, *Of Civil Government*, Bk. II, Ch. VIII, par. 104, p. 168. Apparently Locke conceived of the contract as being actually the historical basis of states. "Reason being plain on our side that men are naturally free; and the examples of history showing that the governments of the world, that were begun in peace, had their beginning laid on that foundation, and were made by the consent of the people; there can be little room for doubt, either where the right is, or what has been the opinion or practice of mankind about the first erecting of governments."

[55] The mediaevalists firmly believed in the actual contractual basis of the state. Carlyle, *op. cit.*, III, 168. "It is, indeed, of the first importance to observe that Manegold's conception is not constructed upon some quasi-historical conception of the beginning of political society, but rather represents in concrete form the constitutional principle of the mediaeval state as embodied in the traditional methods of election or recognition, and of the reciprocal oaths of the coronation ceremonies."

law he reduced to a minimum their method of gaining consent. Tacitly agreeing with them in their concept, he refused to justify the power of the state on that basis. Instead he returned to the broader philosophical principles of Plato and Aristotle.

Burlamaqui wrote that, "man being naturally a free agent, he is capable of making great modification in his primitive state, and of giving by a variety of establishments a new face to human life. Hence those adventitious states are formed, which are properly the work of man, wherein he finds himself placed by his own act, and in consequence of establishments, whereof he himself is the author."[56] Strikingly like Aristotle, Burlamaqui enumerates three "adventitious" states—the family, property, and the state. He differs from Aristotle only in the order of their introduction.[57] According to Burlamaqui the first was "the state of families . . . the most natural and most ancient of all societies, and the very foundation of that which is called national; for the people or nation is only an assemblage or composition of several families." Property was not an inalienable right of man for "all men had originally a right to a common use of whatever the earth produces for their several wants." Admitting, however, the right to property as constituting the second "adventitious state," he said, "this must necessarily arise from some human act; and consequently the state of human property ought to be ranked among the adventitious states." Of all the modifications of natural society by man, one stands in bold relief in relation to all others. "But among all the states established by the act of man, there is none more

[56] *Politic Law*, Pt. I, Ch. IV, par. vi, p. 40.

[57] However, it should be noted that Aristotle recognized historically that the family preceded the state.

considerable than the civil state, or that of civil society and government."[58]

The problem, Burlamaqui wrote, was "to unite forever the wills of all the members of the society, in such a manner that from that time forward they should never desire but one and the same thing in whatever relates to the end and purpose of society."[59]

In contrast to Hobbes and Rousseau the covenant, according to Burlamaqui, created a body politic only. Burlamaqui admitted certain characteristics of personality to the state. However, he vigorously attacked the juristic concept as expounded by Hobbes. He would have opposed strenuously the real personality theory subsequently maintained by Rousseau. It was an impossibility, Burlamaqui said, so to unite by contract the wills of each that the result would be an all-inclusive personality. A covenant "could never be so effected as to actually destroy the natural diversity of inclinations and sentiments of men." It is true, however, that the will of the state and the individual may be identical provided they are both motivated by the same high objectives. That is, he admitted the possibility of uniting the wills of men (conceding the characteristics he ascribed to them) in such a manner that so long as they all desire and strive for the end of society—the good life of each—they will be obeying their own will and the will of the state. This is far from saying, however, that the contract brings into existence an overpowering personality. Burlamaqui accomplished his purpose that everyone should "desire but one and the same thing in whatever relates to the end and purpose of society."

The state exercised some powers similar to those of an

[58] *Natural Law*, Pt. I, Ch. IV, pars. vi, ix, pp. 40, 41.
[59] *Politic Law*, Pt. I, Ch. IV, par. iv, p. 23.

individual. The head of the state acting in behalf of the members thereof could do things peculiar to the position which he occupied. "The state is therefore considered as a body or as a moral person, of which the sovereign is the chief or head, and the subjects are the members; in consequence of which we attribute to this person certain actions peculiar to him, certain rights, privileges, and possessions, distinct from those of each citizen, and to which neither each citizen, nor many, nor even all together, can pretend, but only the sovereign."[60]

This idea of the corporate personality of the state is further conveyed in his definition of the state as a "society by which a multitude of people united together, under the dependence of a sovereign, in order to find, through his protection and care, the happiness to which they naturally aspire." Again, in distinguishing the state from a multitude, "the state is a body, or a society, animated by one only soul, which directs all its motions, and makes all its members act after a constant and uniform manner, with a view to one and the same end, namely, the public utility."[61] Since the original compact could never "actually destroy the natural diversity of inclinations and sentiments of men," since men did not give up natural liberty, since sovereignty always resides "virtually" in the people, since the "seeds" of sovereignty reside in the individual *per se*, then it was impossible for Burlamaqui to assign to the state more than a legal corporate personality existing only because of the necessity arising from its responsibility to the individual.

What is more important, the power of the state, according to Burlamaqui, does not come from the union of the

[60] *Ibid.*, par. x, p. 25.
[61] *Ibid.*, pars. ix-x, pp. 25-26.

wills into one general will, but from the consent of individual wills which always remain individual wills even though they form, together, a united will for the state. The force of the state comes from "the engagement itself, by which individuals have subjected themselves to the command of a sovereign, an engagement which derives a considerable force both from divine authority, and from the sanction of an oath. But as to vicious and ill-disposed minds, on whom these motives make no impression, the strength of the government consists chiefly in the fear of those punishments which the sovereign may inflict upon them, by virtue of the power with which he is invested."[62] The sovereign power to inflict punishments, he explicitly pointed out, came only from the consent of the members of the body politic. Thus he declared, "that the rest of the subjects join their strength with him for this end (for, were it not for this, he would have no more power than the lowest of his subjects), it follows from thence, that it is the ready submission of good subjects that furnishes the sovereign with the means of repressing the insolent, and of maintaining his authority."[63]

In conclusion, Burlamaqui may be marked as one of the first of the modern theorists in that he launched an attack upon the mediaevalist concept of the unnaturalness of the state and declared for a return to the fundamentals of Aristotle. He declared happiness to be a natural and inalienable right of man. He was the last of the natural law philosophers. It may be said that he successfully bridged the gap between ancient and modern political thought. The return of Aristotle to a paramount place in political thinking is indicated clearly in the words of Burlamaqui:

[62] *Ibid.*, par. xii, p. 26.
[63] *Ibid.*, par. xiii, p. 27.

"Since civil liberty therefore is far preferable to that of nature, we may safely conclude that the civil state, which procures this liberty to mankind, is of all human states the most perfect, the most reasonable, and of course the true natural state of man."[64]

[64] *Ibid.*, Ch. III, par. xxvi, p. 19.

2

THE NATURE OF SOVEREIGNTY AND LAW

THE ESSENCE of Burlamaqui's concept of sovereignty approximates Duguit's famous words "social solidarity." To be sure, in discussing the source of sovereignty he attempts to explain it as an emanation, so to speak, of those seeds of sovereignty which are in the individual. In so far as he approaches the matter from this angle, his efforts cannot be said to be more successful than those of his contemporaries in solving what must inevitably remain an insoluble problem—the identification of the individual will with the will expressed in the law. But in his concept of the benevolent, the truly wise ruler who governs for the benefit of the ruled, for the advancement of a social welfare of which the individual's good is a part, he sounds a refreshingly new note. The concept is not unlike one aspect of Rousseau's General Will which is defined as general not only in content but also in purpose.

But Burlamaqui does not resort to verbal play with this vain idea that law is the will of the community. Rather he places sovereignty on the firm basis of social necessity. While he uses the term "liberty," it is to be remembered that he distinguishes it from "independence," in the sense that when I am pursuing "happiness" I am "free." The whole argument may be thus summarized: Social existence is necessary for human happiness; sovereignty is accessory to social existence, one of its inevitable products; therefore, sovereignty is legitimate only when limited, not by a more or less narrow and intensely individual body of supposed "natural rights," but by a much broader principle of social welfare, which alone is its final basis.

1

To Burlamaqui sovereignty is "the right of commanding civil society in the last resort, which right the members of this society have conferred on one and the same person, with a view to preserve order and security in the commonwealth, and, in general, to procure, under his protection and through his care, their own real happiness, and especially the sure exercise of their liberty."[1] By definition all omnipotent and arbitrary power is ruled out. The term sovereignty denotes a limited power—limited by the people who confer it and by the end for which it is established.

He defended this definition of sovereignty by breaking it into its component parts and showing that the nature of sovereignty is the "right of commanding the members of the society, that is, of directing their actions with authority, or with a power of compelling. That this right ought to be that of commanding in the last resort in such a manner, that every private person be obliged to submit, without a power left to any man of resisting. Otherwise, if this authority was not superior to every other upon earth, it could establish no order or security in the commonwealth, though these are the ends for which it was established."

[1] *Politic Law*, Pt. I, Ch. V, par. ii, p. 31.

Sovereignty is never identified with a man. It is a concept, the power of which may be exercised by one man or a group. Sovereignty is indivisible, *i.e.*, "there is no sovereign at all when there are many, because there is no one that commands in the last resort." Sovereignty ceases to be sovereignty and those who exercise it cease to be legitimate rulers when they "lose sight of this end; when they pervert it to their private interests, or caprices, sovereignty then degenerates into tyranny, and ceases to be a legitimate authority."[2] Sovereignty is qualitative as well as quantitative.

Before laying down his concept of the origin and situs of sovereignty, Burlamaqui took occasion to inquire into similar theories of the subject. No one, he observed, had a natural right to rule. "There can be neither sovereignty nor natural and necessary dependence between beings, which by their nature, faculties, and state, have so perfect an equality, that nothing can be attributed to one which is not alike applicable to the other." Neither did he accept the proposition that its origin could be found in the "sole superiority of strength, or an irresistible power . . . as some pretend."

"Those who found the right of prescribing laws on this basis," he declared, "establish an insufficient principle, and which, if rigourously considered, is absolutely false. In fact it does not follow that because I am incapable to resist a person, he has therefore a right to command me, that is, that I am bound to submit to him by virtue of a principle of obligation, and to acknowledge his will as the universal rule of my conduct. . . . For instance, the power that may chance to reside in a malignant being neither invests him with any right to command nor imposes any

2 *Ibid.*, pars. iii-vi, pp. 52-54.

obligation on us to obey, because this is evidently repugnant even to the very idea of right and obligation."[3]

Pufendorf founded sovereignty in the superior excellence of nature. Some men are by nature superior, he asserted, and others are inferior. The former regard the latter as being made to be ruled by them. He arrived at this conclusion through his knowledge of the empire of men over brutes.[4] Burlamaqui rejected this doctrine as being insufficient. "I will acknowledge, if you please, this excellency," he argued, "and agree to it as a truth that I am well convinced of : This is the whole effect that must naturally arise from this hypothesis. But there I will make a halt; and the knowledge that I have of the excellency of a superior being, does not alone afford me a motive sufficient to subject myself to him, and to induce me to abandon my own will in order to take his for my rule." In the absence of other bases Burlamaqui did not concede superior quality as the primary determinant of the right to rule. Even granting this superiority he still demanded to be told "how and in what manner does this being, whom you suppose to surpass me in excellence, intend to conduct himself in regard to me; and by what effects will this superiority of excellence be displayed?"[5]

He, likewise, repudiated the teachings of Barbeyrac that the source of sovereignty was in God. Admitting man to be a creature of God and therefore inferior, it did not follow, Burlamaqui replied, that God "had a right to prescribe laws to us." Moreover, "the irresistible power of the creator might indeed constrain the created"; but this

[3] *Natural Law*, Pt. I, Ch. IX, pars. i-iv, pp. 82-85.

[4] Samuel Pufendorf, *Of the Law of Nature and Nations* (Basil Kennett tr. Oxford, 1710), Bk. I, Ch. VI, p. 11.

[5] *Natural Law*, Pt. I, Ch. IX, par. v, pp. 86, 87.

kind of constraint never established a reasonable obligation "because an obligation of this nature always supposes
the concurrence of the will, and an approbation of an acquiescence on the part of man, from whence a voluntary
submission arises."[6]

After rejecting each of these theories of the right of
sovereignty, he asserted that "the right of sovereignty
arises from a superiority of power, accompanied with wisdom and goodness. I say in the first place *a superiority of
power* because an equality of power . . . excludes all empire
. . . and besides, sovereignty and command would become
useless and of no manner of effect, were they not supported
by a sufficient power. But this is not yet sufficient. This
power ought to be *wise* and *benevolent; Wise,* to know
and to chuse the properest means to make us happy; and
benevolent, to be generally inclinable to use those means
that tend to promote our felicity." These three characteristics must always be present in the ruler. It is not sufficient
that he have only one or two. "As power alone, unaccom-
panied with benevolence, cannot constitute right; so
benevolence, destitute of power and wisdom, is likewise
insufficient for this effect."[7]

As to the situs of sovereignty Burlamaqui accepted the
teachings of the monarchomachs, and of Marsiglio of
Padua, who, in their early attacks upon the absolutist system relying upon natural law and the theory of consent,
proclaimed the doctrine of the sovereignty of the people.
Sovereignty, Burlamaqui argued, originally belonged to
the people; it could not be alienated, nor could they lose it
by prescription. Consent is the only basis upon which
legitimate authority may be established. "Sovereignty re-

[6] *Ibid.,* par. vi, p. 86.
[7] *Ibid.,* pars. viii, lx, pp. 90-93.

sides originally in the people, and in each individual with regard to himself; and that it is the transferring and uniting the several rights of individuals in the person of the sovereign that constitutes him such, and really produces sovereignty."[8]

Governments derive their just powers from the consent of the governed. Each individual in the state of nature is possessed of the faculty of sovereignty. It is a latent power because all others possessed the same faculty and to the same degree. Each man can, however, consent to forego the exercise of this faculty. "Since every individual has a natural right of disposing of his natural freedom according as he thinks proper," he asks, "why should he not have the power of transferring to another that right which he has of directing himself? Now is it not manifest that if all the members of this society agree to transfer this right to one of their fellow-members, this cession will be the nearest and immediate cause of sovereignty? It is therefore evident that there are, in each individual, the seeds, as it were, of the supreme power. The case is here very near the same as in that of several voices, collected together, which, by their union, produce a harmony that was not to be found separately in each."[9] Again he asserted: "It is true that neither each member of the society, nor the whole multitude collected, are formally invested with the supreme authority, such as we behold it in the sovereign, but it is sufficient that they possess it virtually, that is, that they have within themselves all that is necessary to enable them, by the concurrence of their free will and consent, to produce it in the sovereign."[10]

[8] *Politic Law*, Pt. 1, Ch. VI, pars. v, vi, pp. 38, 39.
[9] *Ibid.*, par. xv, p. 42.
[10] *Ibid.*, par. xiv.

The uniqueness of Burlamaqui's concept of sovereignty is more clearly demonstrated in his distinction between limited and absolute sovereignty. As Hobbes saw limited sovereignty a contradiction in terms, Burlamaqui saw absolute sovereignty, in the sense of arbitrary power, a contradiction in terms. A fundamental difference between Burlamaqui and Locke is also manifest.

Burlamaqui's discussion of absolute sovereignty is a restatement of Locke's concept of sovereignty. The exercise of this power is limited only by the right of revolution. Conceding the ruler absolute sovereignty "it does not follow," the former reasoned, "that they (the people) have reserved to themselves in no case the right of resuming it. This reservation is sometimes explicit; but there is always a tacit one, the effect of which discloses itself when the person, entrusted with the supreme authority, perverts it to an use directly contrary to the end for which it was conferred upon him."[11]

Absolute sovereignty cannot be synonymous with arbitrary, despotic, and unlimited authority. Sovereignty must by definition, Burlamaqui held, be less than omnicompetence. It is always and inescapably limited by its purpose. To secure the happiness of the individual members of society is its final end. With this as its sole *raison d'être* "how is it possible to conceive that those, who, with this view, granted an absolute power to the sovereign, should have intended to give him an arbitrary and unlimited power?" Always the people "insist upon the sovereign's using his authority for their advantage, and according to the purposes for which he was entrusted with it." Moreover, arbitrary and despotic power can not be

[11] *Ibid.*, Ch. VII, par. xiv, p. 48.

legitimate because it ignores the requirement of social utility. "The very nature of the thing [sovereignty] does not allow absolute power to be extended beyond the bounds of public utility; for absolute sovereignty cannot confer a right upon the sovereign, which the people had not originally in themselves. Now before the establishment of civil society, surely no man had a power of injuring either himself or others; consequently, absolute power cannot give the sovereign a right to hurt and abuse his subjects. It was never the intention of the people to confer absolute sovereignty upon a prince but with this express condition, that the public good should be the supreme law to direct him."[12] The inalienable rights of man are never prescriptible; and, since "absolute power is formed only by the union of all the rights of individuals in the person of the sovereign, of course the absolute power of the sovereign is confined within the same bounds, as those by which the absolute power of individuals was originally limited."[13]

But Burlamaqui was not content with rejecting the identity between absolutism and unlimited authority. He, likewise, rejected absolutism, "limited" absolutism, as he had defined it, as a proper form of governmental organization.

"Absolute power," he wrote, "easily degenerates into despotism, and despotism paves the way for the greatest and most fatal revolutions that can happen to sovereigns." After all, those in power are human with all the desires, passions, and weaknesses of other men, and the temptations are multiplied. Admittedly the people had the natural right to revolt. But in practice this was an unstable reed upon which to lean. Therefore, Burlamaqui recommended

---

[12] *Ibid.*, pars. xviii-xx, pp. 50-51.
[13] *Ibid.*, par. xxi, p. 52.

vigorously the establishment of limited sovereignty. "These reflections, justified by experience, have induced most, and those the wisest nations, to set bounds to the power of their sovereigns, and to prescribe the manner in which the latter are to govern; and this has produced what is called limited sovereignty."[14]

Limited sovereignty signifies restrictions imposed by the body politic separate and distinct from those of natural law. The body politic for its own defense sets up specific rules which serve as deterrents to an errant government and as guides to wise ones. The rules are simply additional precautions taken by the people to insure the accomplishment of the end for which sovereignty was established. "These regulations, by which the supreme authority is kept within bounds, are called the *fundamental laws of the state*."[15]

2

Contractual philosophy had proceeded from the thesis of the natural freedom of man to be governed by his own will to the conclusion that legitimate law was binding because it, in one way or another, was still the individual's own will. Hobbes, Locke, and Rousseau, however different in other respects, were in agreement that this was the problem and the answer. Thus they were as one in emphasizing that the right to make law was determined by the source of the rule and, as a corollary, that all rules emanating from that source were binding. To be sure, Locke sought to set limits beyond which the representative legislature could not go, but true law was binding just

---

[14] *Ibid.*, pars. xxx-xxxiv, pp. 54-55.
[15] *Ibid.*, par. xxxv, p. 55. See also Ch. III, *infra.*

because it was a rule made by a majority of a miniature community. The majority had the right to rule. Rousseau, too, recognized that the people might sometimes err and so issue unjust rules. But in general the proposition holds good that the three philosophers found justice to lie in the source from which the rule proceeded.

The thoroughly juristic Hobbes asserted that the problem was one of reducing the many wills to a single will. This, he contended, was accomplished by the social contract. This problem of the relation of sovereign-government to sovereign-body politic or state was solved by Hobbes through the concept of legal personality. The social compact created an inchoate person, the state. A choice of a governmental sovereign, one or plural, to wield as his that sovereignty was necessary to give this state person *real* unity. Thus the action of the sovereign was, legally, the act of the body politic, getting its binding authority from the body politic, which, by the terms of the contract, had absolute power to rule.[16]

With Locke, the situation is clouded by the fact that he sought to give expression in his theory to two really incompatible ideas. On the one hand, Locke unmistakably held that government and body politic were distinct, and the former, including the supreme legislature, was in a fiduciary relation to the latter. This points in the direction of a fundamental law which is the people's charter of powers to government. But as a matter of fact, Locke scarcely reached the conception of a legislature controlled other than by an ultimate right of revolution. His legislature, although not unlimited, was nonetheless sovereign in the sense in which the community was sovereign, being

---

[16] *Leviathan*, Bk. II, Ch. XVII, p. 89.

limited only because, and insofar as, the community was limited. For Locke was not only interested in the question of what laws may not be made, but also why man, *ex hypothesi* with a natural freedom of self-direction, should obey any law. And the only answer that he can find is in reality that of Hobbes and Rousseau: law is binding as the expression of your own will as a member of the political community. But Locke maintained that only law made by a representative assembly had such a character. "And thus the commonwealth," he wrote, "comes by a power to set down what punishment shall belong to the several transgressions they think worthy of it, committed amongst the members of that society (which is the power of making laws), as well as it has the power to punish any injury done unto any of its members by any one that is not of it (which is the power of war and peace); and all this for the preservation of the property of all the members of that society, as far as is possible."[17]

Indeed, as is frequently ignored by commentators, Locke incorporated the basic idea of Hobbes' juristic person. "But though every man entered into society has quitted his power to punish offences against the law of Nature in prosecution of his own private judgment, yet with the judgment of offences which he has given up to the legislative, in all cases where he can appeal to the magistrate, he has given up a right to the commonwealth to employ his force for the execution of the judgments of the commonwealth whenever he shall be called to it, which indeed, are his own judgments, they being made by himself or his representative."[18] This is a clear enough statement of

[17] *Of Civil Government*, Bk. II, Ch. VII, par. 88, p. 159.
[18] *Ibid.*, p. 160.

the complete identity between the will of the legislature
and the individual members of the community.

Burlamaqui, on the contrary, was one of the early ob-
jectivists. He sought the binding force of law in its content
principally rather than its source. He emphasized the
qualitative nature of sovereignty as the determinant of its
legitimacy and relegated to secondary importance the
source or the purely juristic characteristic. Law existed,
he declared, solely as a rational and social rule. The binding force of law must be determined always by the stand-
ards prescribed by right reason and social utility. He held
that law in a general sense is all that directs, but he added,
that "law is everything that the reason recognizes as a
sure and necessary means of arriving at happiness." [19]

In source there are two classifications of law, he wrote,
" (1) With respect to their authority only, and (2) with
regard to their original. To the former class we refer all
the natural laws which serve as rules in civil courts, and
which are also confirmed by a new sanction of the sovereign." As to the latter, their foundation is "only the will
of the sovereign, and suppose certain human establishments; or which regulate things relating to the particular
advantage of the state, though indifferent in themselves,
and undetermined by the law of nature." [20]

These categories of law become merged in one so far
as the laying of obligation is concerned. Obviously, this
would be true when he made no essential difference between civil and natural society. "The primitive and natural state of man may admit of different changes and modifications, which are left to the disposal of man, and have
nothing contrary to his obligations and duties. In this re-

[19] See Leon Duguit, *Traite de droit constitutionnel*, I, 24, 205.
[20] *Politic Law*, Pt. III, Ch. I, pars. vii, viii, p. 155.

spect, the civil laws may produce a few changes in the natural state, and consequently make some regulations unknown to the law of nature, without containing anything contrary to that law, which supposes the state of liberty in its full extent, but nevertheless, permits mankind to limit and restrain that state in the manner which appears most to their advantage." [21] The state of society was, to him, the natural state of man. Hence all man-made or acquired law was of necessity in conformity with natural law. Thus the obligations to obey the one were the same as the obligations to obey the other.

Man owes obedience to law because of an internal obligation or "that which is produced only by our reason, considered as the primitive rule of conduct, and in consequence of the good or evil the action in itself contains." [22] "Conscience," he explained, "is properly no more than reason itself, considered as instructed in regard to the rule we ought to follow, or the law of nature." Continuing further, he indicated that one sometimes uses the word "conscience" to characterize a judgment. In order better to interpret reason and its operation, he said that a "person compares two propositions, one of which includes the law, and the other action; and from thence he deduces a third; which is the judgment he makes of the quality of his action." Moreover, "it is not sufficient for a judge to be well acquainted with the tenor and purport of law, before he pronounces sentence; he should likewise have an exact knowledge of the fact and all its different circumstances." [23] Thus an enlightened conscience is the only "sure rule of conduct whose dictates may be followed with

[21] *Ibid.*, par. xi, p. 157.
[22] *Natural Law*, Pt. I, Ch. VI, par. xiii, p. 66.
[23] *Ibid.*, Pt. II, Ch. IX, pars. ii-iv, pp. 226-27.

a perfect confidence." In the words of a modern writer, the moral personality of man is such that he "is irresistibly impelled to formulate for himself an ideal of perfection toward the attainment of which he is conscious of a moral obligation to strive." [24] Therefore, the ultimate choice which man's reason dictates is determined by the end. That is, it must determine whether the act is compatible with the fullest development of the ideal self.

The importance of the purpose of the law is further emphasized by the first characteristic which Burlamaqui maintained a law must possess in order to lay an internal obligation—the content. It may be contended that he made no particular contribution beyond that of Locke in the previous century; for Locke had specifically stated that laws promulgated by the sovereign must conform to natural law. But Burlamaqui had a more comprehensive meaning than merely conforming to natural law. For the content of law must not only meet this test, but it must "contribute to the particular good of each person, to that of society in general, and to the glory of the sovereign. This supposes naturally that the things ordained by the law be possible to fulfill"; that it must be socially useful and finally "be itself just." Reason does not demand that men obey law "without any benefit or advantage arising to them." No law is put over man merely "for the sake of restraint." The law thus is positive in nature. In this important respect he departed radically from the contractualist concept of law as a negative rule. [25]

Another characteristic of law is external obligation; by which is meant "that which arises from the will of a being on whom we allow ourselves dependent, and who

[24] Willoughby, *op. cit.*, p. 242.
[25] *Natural Law*, Pt. 1, Ch. X, pars. viii, iv, p. 103.

commands or prohibits some particular things, under a combination of punishment." [26] Hence, the law must be made public. It was not enough for the law-giver to be vague in specifications. Law is a rule which distinguishes it from counsel which is not obligatory. To produce an external obligation law has to be "attended with a proper sanction." [27] Therefore he concluded, "for as men are framed, the laws derive their greatest force from the coercive power which, by exemplary punishments, intimidates the wicked, and balances the superior force of pleasure and passion." [28]

The last characteristic of binding laws is "the authority of the sovereign that prescribes them." Although defining law in the conventional manner of the contractualists as "a rule prescribed by the sovereign of a society to his subjects" he did not contend that this was alone sufficient to establish obligation.[29] He might define law in the same terminology of the contractual school but it must be remembered that he defined sovereignty in terms of its content.

Burlamaqui agreed that consent was necessary to, or was a basis of the obligation to obey law. He assumed that through covenant man had submitted "his private will to that of a single person, or assembly," but, he asked, to what extent had man yielded his private will? Only in so far, he replied, as the rules of the sovereign "concerned things relative to the public security or advantage," and only in these respects can it be "considered as the positive will of all in general, and of each in particular." [30]

[26] *Ibid.*, Ch. VI, par. xiii, p. 66.
[27] *Ibid.*, Ch. X, par. x, p. 104.
[28] *Politic Law*, Pt. I, Ch. III, par. viii, p. 13.
[29] *Natural Law*, Pt. I, Ch. VIII, pars. iii-v, pp. 78-79.
[30] *Politic Law*, Pt. I, Ch. IV, par. vi, p. 24.

Since Burlamaqui required that law proceed only from legitimate governments, he was forced to seek an answer to the question, "Which is the most legitimate government?" "It is certain," his response ran, "that governments of every kind, which are founded on the free acquiescence of the people, whether express or justified by a long and peaceable possession, are all equally legitimate, so long at least as, by the intention of the sovereign, they tend to promote the happiness of the people." [31] He distinguished a "best government" and a "legitimate government." The one does not necessarily imply the other. The basis of each may be entirely different. Only a legitimate government establishes obligation; and then only within specified limitations. In laying an external obligation the government takes cognizance of the content of law, not only as Locke had contended by not violating the laws of nature, but also by not subverting sovereignty "to their private interests, or caprices; sovereignty then degenerates into tyranny, and ceases to be a legitimate authority." [32] Moreover, the fundamental laws had to be satisfied in the content of the law of the sovereign. No law contrary to the constitution establishes an obligation of obedience.

Thus, he concluded: "As the external obligation is capable of giving a new force to the internal, so the whole force of the external obligation ultimately depends on the internal; and it is from the agreement and concurrence of these two obligations . . . that the most perfect obligation is found." [33]

[31] *Ibid.*, Pt. II, Ch. II, par. xiii, p. 87.
[32] *Ibid.*, Pt. I, Ch. V, par. vi, pp. 52 ff.
[33] *Natural Law*, Pt. I, Ch. VI, par. viii, p. 66.

3

CONSTITUTIONAL GOVERNMENT

THE GENERAL concept of government limited by a higher law, whether denominated, divine, or natural, is of great antiquity. It was in the seventeenth and eighteenth centuries, however, that the concept became the accepted philosophy of the rising middle class in its struggle against feudalism and monarchical government. Limited government became the dogma of this newly conscious class in demanding its seat at the political controls. The basic tenet of this new political philosophy was the doctrine of a law of nature which was superior to all man-made law. Its maxim was the doctrine of inalienable, natural rights and the glorification of the individual. Under the banner of limited or constitutional government imposing names parade across the span of two centuries—among others Grotius, Pufendorf, Hooker, Coke, Roger Williams, Locke and Montesquieu. In this illustrious group one name stands out above all others as the great liberal and constitutionalist—John Locke. He, the apologist of the Glorious Revolution, proclaimed the philosophical right of revolution on the fundamental law of nature.

It is generally accepted that the philosophy of Locke furnished the theoretic basis for the American theory of constitutional government. It may, however, be confidently asserted that it is impossible logically to deduce from Locke's doctrine such characteristically American principles as the written constitution, as the people's grant of power to government, personal separation of powers, coordinate departments, checks and balances, limited legislative power—except as limited by the natural rights of life, liberty, and property—and, most American of them all, judicial review. Instead, the earliest theoretic statement of these principles as a systematized method of government, with the exception of the last, which was at least adumbrated, is contained in Burlamaqui's *Principes du droit naturel,* 1747.

It is not to be maintained that Burlamaqui, any more than Locke, originated the concept that the state was not possessed of unlimited power. It may be maintained, however, that Burlamaqui was one of the first political philosophers to conceive of governmental power limited by a fundamental constitution distinct from the law of nature.

1

In the early seventeenth century Coke had written of a higher law controlling upon parliament. In substance this higher law was nothing more than the law of nature. In reporting Calvin's Case, he summarized his concept of fundamental law to this effect: "1. That legeance or obedience of the subject to the sovereign is due to the law of nature: 2. That this law of nature is part of the laws of England: 3. That the law of nature is before any judicial or municipal law in the world: 4. That the law of nature is immutable, and cannot be changed." [1] It appears quite

[1] Calvin's Case, 7 Coke R. 46 (1610), quoted in Edward S. Corwin, "The 'Higher Law' Background of American Constitutional Law," *Harvard Law Review,* XLII (December, 1928; January, 1929), 149, 365.

evident that he had no comprehension of a body of fundamental law emanating from the body politic in its sovereign capacity. Only because of policy were laws considered controlling. It is dangerous, he observed, to change the ancient laws of the realm. The rule of policy applied whether the law was an act of parliament, a common law, or a custom. [2] Over all other rules Coke exalted the common law. Its source was judge-made decisions based upon reason and justice—in content no different from natural law. Coke did not anticipate the subsequent American rule for determining fundamental law, namely, its source.

Coke's assumption of a higher law laid the groundwork upon which Locke, in the latter part of the same century, asserted the ethical justification of the right of revolution and the philosophical theory of limited state and government. The central thesis of Locke's philosophy being the ethical basis for revolt, he took the broader philosophical concept of the law of nature rather than Coke's more narrow legal notion of acts of parliament, customs, or the common law. Locke's thoughts concerning constitutional government were incidental to his major proposition, the right of revolution. Reasserting the principle of popular sovereignty as a basic tenet of the social contract theory, after its subversion by Hobbes, Locke enunciated the doctrine of limited state and government. Apprehending vaguely a second contract between the body politic and the ruler, he declared all governmental power to be fiduciary in nature.[3]

[2] R. A. MacKay, "Coke—Parliamentary Sovereignty or the Supremacy of the Law?" *Michigan Law Review*, XXII (January, 1924), 215.

[3] *Of Civil Government*, Bk. II, Ch. XIII, par. 149, p. 192: "There can be but one supreme power, which is the legislative . . . yet the legislative being only a fiduciary power to act for certain ends, there remains still in the people a supreme power to remove or alter the legislative."

Locke's failure to distinguish clearly between the original and the governmental contract resulted in his differentiating state and government in concept but not in power. The logical conclusion of this reasoning was an identity in the power of the state and government in both content and degree. In concept the totality of political power residing in the body politic was distinguished from governmental power in that it was original while the latter was delegated. Actually the government had all the power of the body politic. The government could do anything the state could do. It was limited only by those forces which circumscribed the authority of the body politic. Also, the legislature was supreme. It was all-powerful within the confines of the law of nature. In no instance did Locke suggest any specific limitations upon the government which were not imposed upon the state. Evidently, this is not the American doctrine of limited government.

Locke's fundamental law was natural law. The establishment of a legislature is the "first and fundamental natural law which is to govern even the legislative." [4] In one instance only did he use the word "positive" to characterize this law. It appears rather evident that he had not broken with the tradition of Coke and earlier writers. He made no real distinction between natural and positive law. [5]

Locke did not propose a theory of government limited in power beyond the restrictions upon the state which created it. Natural law and, subordinate to it, the end of

[4] *Ibid.*, Ch. XI, par. 134, p. 183.
[5] Herbert D. Foster, *Collected Papers*, p 164. The idea is here developed that Hooker, Grotius, Locke, Buchanan and others had no understanding of a controlling law not identified with natural law.

political society were binding alike upon both. If those in
authority subverted either, the people might refuse submission and in the last analysis withdraw their mandate
and through the right of revolution change the form of
government. "For all power given with trust for the attaining of an end being limited by that end," he declared,
"whenever that end is manifestly neglected or opposed,
the trust must necessarily be forfeited, and the power dis-
solve into the hands of those that gave it, who may place it
anew where they shall think it best for their safety and
security. And thus the community perpetually retains a
supreme power of saving themselves from the attempts
and designs of any body, even of their legislators, whenever they shall be so foolish or so wicked as to lay and
carry on designs against the liberties and properties of the
subject." [6] The body politic had the law of nature only,
but always, to depend upon as the immediate and final
protector of its rights. Such law "stands as an eternal
rule to all men, legislators as well as others . . . and the
fundamental law of Nature being the preservation of
mankind, no human sanction can be good or valid against
it." [7]

Burlamaqui succeeded, as Locke failed, in constructing
the purely American constitutional principle of a funda-

[6] *Of Civil Government*, Bk. II, Ch. XIII, par. 149, p. 192.

[7] *Ibid.*, Ch. XI, par. 135, p. 185. See also Ch. XIX, par. 222, p. 229.
"Whensoever, therefore, the legislative shall transgress this fundamental
law of society, and either by ambition, fear, folly, or corruption, endeavour
to grasp themselves, or put into the hands of any other, an absolute power
over the lives, liberties, and estates of the people, by this breach of trust they
forfeit the power the people had put into their hands for quite contrary ends,
and it devolves to the people, who have a right to resume their original
liberty, and by the establishment of a new legislative (such as they shall
think fit), provide for their own safety and security, which is the end for
which they are in society."

mental law as separate and distinct from the law of nature. Agreeing with Locke that the totality of all political power resides in the body politic, Burlamaqui asserted that there were basic reasons, however, why the government should not be possessed of the same power. He was not willing to rest his case solely upon the law of nature, and insisted that additional restrictions be placed upon the government through the fundamental law. This concept is implicit in his concept of law and sovereignty. At this point Burlamaqui stands out in bold relief from the contractualists.

The importance of Burlamaqui's concept to American constitutional theory is evident. It lies in the fact that his position made possible the limitation of the powers of government without, in turn, restricting to the same degree the power of the state. This was a new doctrine in political science. It advanced the idea of a fundamental law—a constitution—emanating from the sovereign body politic, which was superior to all man-made law; a fundamental law which was the source of all governmental power and which imposed limitations upon government in addition to those of the law of nature.[8] Burlamaqui's basic law was thus quite different from that proposed by Locke and Coke.

To be sure Burlamaqui recognized the existence of a higher law which was binding upon both state and government and superior to the constitution. But under this higher law he held the rulers to be bound only morally to do right and to govern in the interest of the people. The body politic, he asserted, had the right of revolution only as a final sanction. Burlamaqui distinguished intelligibly between the law of nature and the constitution as funda-

[8] See *infra* Ch. VI.

mental law, as in the following: "I observe in the first place that there is a kind of fundamental law, essential to all government, even in those states where the most absolute sovereignty prevails. This law is that of the public good, from which the sovereign can never depart, without being wanting in his duty; but this alone is not sufficient to limit sovereignty." This law is founded on "promises, either tacit or express ... and ... does not imply any limitation to their authority, nor diminution of their absolute power." [9] This is the "Higher Law" doctrine of the American constitution.

Again distinguishing in concept and in power a fundamental law issuing from the body politic and the "Higher Law," he argued: "With regard to fundamental laws, properly so called, they are only more particular precautions taken by the people, to oblige sovereigns more strongly to employ their authority agreeably to the general rule of the public good." [10] Under this theory the doctrine of delegated authority becomes an actual limitation upon governmental power. The body politic delegated to the government only that quantity of power which it deemed essential for the well-being of the members of the state. The government was an agent of the state; it had a specific grant of authority which constrained its actions within the confines of the fundamental law. The rulers under this form of government, he declared, are "properly no more than the executors of the law, since it is from the law itself that they hold their power." [11]

The fundamental law or constitution is not to be con-

[9] *Politic Law*, Pt. I, Ch. VII, pars. xxxix, xl, pp. 56-57.
[10] *Ibid.*, par. xli, p. 57.
[11] *Ibid.*, Pt. II, Ch. I, par. xxii, p. 75.

fused with a mere covenant. It is *legally* binding between the parties to the contract. "The fundamental laws of a state," Burlamaqui argued, "taken in their full extent, are not only the decrees by which the entire body of the nation determine the form of government, and the manner of succeeding to the crown; but are likewise the covenants betwixt the people and the person on whom they confer the sovereignty, which regulate the manner of governing, and by which the supreme authority is limited. . . . But as those covenants are obligatory between the contracting parties, they have the force of laws themselves." [12] A fundamental law is the process through which the body politic grants and thus limits governmental power. It is a method of protecting the liberties of the people from arbitrary control. The basic characteristic of the fundamental laws is the source, "because they are the basis, as it were, and foundation of the state, on which the structure of the government is raised, and because the people look upon these regulations as their principal strength and support."

In extreme cases the body politic could always fall back upon the law of nature in defense of its rights. As a matter of practical concern, however, the body politic should establish a fundamental law. It constitutes a bulwark against the growth of unlimited and arbitrary power in the hands of the rulers. The imposition of checks to the abuse of authority is a far saner, safer, and more practical proposition than relying upon the right of revolution to regain that which had been usurped. In further defense of the theory of limited government, he declared: "It is by such precautions as these, that a nation really limits the author-

[12] *Ibid.*, Pt. I, Ch. VII, pars. xxxvi-xxxviii, pp. 55-56.

ity she confers on the sovereign, and secures her liberty. For . . . civil liberty ought to be accompanied not only with a right of insisting on the sovereign's making a use of his authority, but moreover with a moral certainty that his right shall have its effect. And the only way to render the people thus certain, is to use proper precautions against the abuse of the sovereign power, in such a manner as these precautions shall not be easily eluded." [13]

The nature of the constitution, he wrote, was both positive and negative. It was positive in that it contained specific grants of power to the government. It was negative in that certain powers were specifically prohibited. Also it was negative in the fact that an enumeration of powers constituted a limitation upon the exercise of governmental authority. This is basic to American Constitutionalism. The fundamental law is such, he wrote, that a "nation may require of a sovereign, that he will engage, by a particular promise, not to make any new laws, not to lay new imposts, to tax only some particular things, to give places and employments to a certain set of people, and not take any foreign troops into his pay, etc." [14]

The constitution conceived by Burlamaqui was truly in the American sense fundamental. It came from the people. It was the source of all governmental power. The fiduciary relationship of the government to the state was actual. The constitution could be amended only by the body politic.

"In a word, the constitution of those governments can be changed," he observed, "only in the same manner, and by the same methods, by which it was established, that is

13 *Ibid.*, par. xliv, p. 59.
14 *Ibid.*, par. xlii, p. 57.

to say by the unanimous concurrence of all the contracting parties who have fixed the form of government by the
original contract." [15] This is orthodox American doctrine
and practice. The binding character of fundamental law
is further emphasized by Burlamaqui's assertion that
under no circumstances, no matter how extenuating,
could the government violate the constitution. To permit
this practice would be to subvert the principle of popular
sovereignty. "But if there should happen to be an extra-
ordinary case," he wrote, "in which the sovereign
thought it conclusive to the public good, to deviate from
the fundamental laws, he is not allowed to do it of his
head, in contempt of the solemn engagement, but in that
case he ought to consult the people themselves, or their
representatives. Otherwise, under pretence of some necessity or utility, the sovereign might easily break his word,
and frustrate the effect of the precautions taken by the
nation to limit his power." [16]

Anticipating the American idea of making and changing fundamental law, he proposed that the constitution
establish the procedure by which power could be added:
"But, for a still greater security of the performance of the
engagements into which the sovereign entered, and which
limit his power, it is proper to require explicitly of him,
that he shall convene a general assembly of the people, or
of their representatives . . . when any matters happen to
fall under debate, which it was thought improper to leave
to his decision." Moreover, he suggested that the constitution might establish a particular institution for perform-
ing this particular function in the form of a "council, a

[15] *Ibid.*, Pt. II, Ch. I, par. xxiv, p. 76.
[16] *Ibid.*, Pt. I, Ch. VII, par. xlii, pp. 57-58.

senate, or parliament, without whose consent the prince shall be rendered incapable of acting in regard to things which the nation did not think fit to submit to his will." [17]

2

The constitutional principles of separation of powers and checks and balances as limiting controls upon government followed logically from the development of the constitution as a fundamental grant of power. The separation of delegated authority into the three rather generally accepted functions of government he proposed as a further limiting principle. This was the particular method of gaining more specific control over the government. This scheme of delegating authority was peculiarly adapted to the prevention of the growth of concentrated authority. This proposal was indeed but a refinement of the broader concept of delegated power.

As a limiting principle, separation of powers had been proposed by many political philosophers. However, the peculiarly American adaptation of it in the eighteenth century was not well known nor so ancient in origin. The characteristically American principle of the separation of powers, functionally and personally, into coördinate departments was set forth by Burlamaqui. [18]

It is true that Locke had stated the rule of separation. But it was not the American concept. In the first place, he did not conceive of delegated authority as a limiting force upon government separate and distinct from the law of

[17] *Ibid.*, p. 58.
[18] B. F. Wright, Jr. "The Origin of the Separation of Powers in America," *Economica*, XIII (May, 1935), 185. The idea is developed that it is purely American in origin—the result of practices of over a century.

nature. He had no occasion then to announce this principle as an added guarantee to the liberties of the people. Secondly, he did not propose a constitution which contained a limited grant of power from the body politic to the government. Therefore, no basis existed for a separation of power into coördinate departments.

The legislature, established by covenant, was given the totality of all power possessed by the state. "The first and fundamental positive law of all commonwealths," Locke wrote, "is the establishing of the legislative power. . . . The Legislative is not only the supreme power of the commonwealth, but sacred and unalterable in the hands where the community have once placed it. Nor can any edict of anybody else, in what form soever conceived, or by what power soever backed, have the force and obligation of a law which has not its sanction from that which the public has chosen and appointed. . . ." [19] Moreover, Locke made no provision at this time for other departments. It is to be concluded that the legislature was the only branch created by the compact.

Locke's doctrine eventuates in a supreme legislature, possessed of the plenitude of governmental power, and limited only by the body of natural rights, which in the last analysis were enforceable by revolution.

The principle of functional separation was introduced by necessity—to expedite the working of government. No limiting rule of government was attached to it. He suggested a functional separation into legislative and executive "because the laws that are at once, and in a short time made, have a constant and lasting force, and need a perpetual execution, or an attendance thereunto, therefore

[19] *Of Civil Government*, Bk. II, Ch. XI, par. 134, pp. 183, 184.

it is necessary there should be a power always in being which should see to the execution of the laws that are made, and remain in force. And thus the legislative and executive power came often to be separated." [20] The executive was created because of expedience—for by the very nature of the legislature it did not remain in session continuously and unless someone was designated to continue the execution of the laws, they would not be properly enforced.

The important aspect of Locke's concept of the executive with which we are concerned is the source of its power. It was not created by the original act which set up the supreme legislature. It cannot, therefore, be conceived as deriving its authority from the same source. The logical conclusion is that the source of all executive power was the legislature. To this effect he wrote that "in a constituted commonwealth standing upon its own basis and acting according to its own nature . . . there can be but one supreme power, which is the legislative, to which all the rest are and must be subordinate." [21] As if this statement did not show clearly the subordinate position of the executive, he continues, "the executive power placed anywhere but in a person that has also a share in the legislative is visibly subordinate and accountable to it, and may be at pleasure changed and displaced; so that it is not the supreme executive power that is exempt from subordination, but the supreme executive power vested in one, who having a share in the legislative, has no distinct superior legislative to be subordinate and accountable to, farther than he himself shall join and consent." [22]

[20] *Ibid.*, Ch. XII, par. 144, pp. 190-91.
[21] *Ibid.*, par. 149, p. 192.
[22] *Ibid.*, Ch. XIII, par. 152, p. 194.

In one respect only can the executive be considered as independent. "In some commonwealths," Locke said, "where the legislative is not always in being, and the executive is vested in a single person who has also a share in the legislative, there that single person, in a very tolerable sense, may also be called supreme; not that he has in himself supreme power, which is that of law-making, but because he has in him the supreme execution from whom all inferior magistrates derive all their several subordinate powers, or at least, the greatest part of them; having also no legislative superior to him, there being no law to be made without his consent, which cannot be expected should ever subject him to the other part of the legislative, he is properly enough in this sense supreme. But yet it is to be observed that though oaths of allegiance and fealty are taken to him, it is not to him as supreme legislator, but as supreme executor of the law made by a joint power of him with others, allegiance being nothing but an obedience according to law, which, when he violates, he has no right to obedience, nor can claim it otherwise than as the public person vested with the power of the law, and so is to be considered as the image, phantom, or representative of the commonwealth . . . and thus he has no will, no power, but that of law." [23]

Locke thus negated any idea of personal separation of powers, any idea of a functional separation as establishing a limitation, and the concept of coördinate departments. He applied the word "supreme" to the executive in a purely superficial manner, when he said that he was "to be considered as the image, phantom, or representative of the commonwealth . . . and thus he has no will, no power, but that of law." As an administrative officer of the legis-

[23] *Ibid.*, par. 151, pp. 193, 194.

lature, the executive may be termed "supreme" within
the law which is an emanation of the supreme legislature.
His concept of the supreme legislature is again emphasized: "When the legislative hath put the execution of the
laws they make into other hands, they have a power still to
resume it out of those hands when they find cause, and to
punish for any maladministration against the laws. The
same holds also in regard to the federative power, that and
the executive being both ministerial and subordinate to
the legislative which, as has been shown, the legislative
also in this case being supposed to consist of several persons; for if it be a single person it cannot but be always in
being, and so will, as supreme, naturally have the supreme
executive power, together with the legislative. . . ." [24]

Locke advocated a functional separation of governmental power into a supreme legislature and a subordinate
executive existing only for expediency. He did not propose a system of coördinate departments, personal separation of powers and, consequently, no principle of checks
and balances.

Burlamaqui, on the contrary, effected a constitutional
principle which was an added limitation to governmental
authority. He was not content to allow governmental limitation to rest solely upon a *concept* of fundamental law.
This, it is true, restricted the powers of the rulers. But, he
maintained, to make this delegation properly effective, a
particular type of delegation is needed. The general grant
of power in the constitution must be separated into coordinate departments. In addition, governmental powers
must be divided both functionally and personally. He
stated clearly this constitutional principle as follows:

[24] *Ibid.*, par. 153, pp. 194, 195.

"There is still another manner of limiting the authority of those to whom the sovereignty is committed; which is not to trust all the different rights included in the sovereignty to one single person, but to lodge them in separate hands, or in different bodies, that they may modify or restrain the sovereignty." [25]

How explicitly Burlamaqui summarized the principles of popular sovereignty, delegation of authority, the constitution as a fundamental law, and the true American doctrine of separation of powers is further shown in the following: "But this union of the supreme power does not hinder the whole body of the nation, in whom this power originally resides, from regulating the government by a fundamental law, in such a manner as to commit the exercise of the different parts of the supreme power to different persons or bodies, who may act independently of each other, in regard to the rights committed to them, but still subordinate to the laws from which those rights are derived." [26] The departments established by the constitution are allocated special powers; and with regard to its authority each department may act "independently" of the others. Each, also, has the power of preserving itself from the encroachments of the others. Neither of the departments is supreme for they are always "subordinate to the laws from which those rights are derived." This is orthodox American doctrine. Moreover, it is not enough, he said, to separate power into different branches and place it in different hands, but a clear line of demarcation must be drawn between the departments "so that we may easily see the extent of their jurisdiction."

To drive home the American constitutional principle of

[25] *Politic Law*, Pt. I, Ch. VII, par. xlviii, p. 61.
[26] *Ibid.*, Pt. II, Ch. I, par. xix, p. 75.

separation of powers into coördinate branches with the
constitution as the sole source of authority, he wrote:
"Thus what constitutes the characteristic of mixed or
compound commonwealths, and distinguishes them from
simple governments, is, that the different orders of the
state, who have a share in the sovereignty, possess the
rights which they exercise by an equal title, that is to say,
in virtue of the fundamental law, and not under the title
of commission, as if one was only the minister or executor of the other's will." [27] To the same effect, he had said:
"They, who thus share the sovereignty among them, are
properly no more than the executors of the law, since it
is from the law itself that they hold their power." [28]

As to the various departments into which governmental
power should be divided, the political philosophers were
not in agreement. Locke conceived of only two functions,
legislative and executive, although he divided the latter
into executive and federative. By the executive he understood "the execution of the municipal laws of the society
within itself upon all that are parts of it." By federative
he comprehended the control of foreign relations or "the
management of the security and interest of the public
without." [29]

Montesquieu, on the other hand, made a clear division
of governmental power into three branches: legislative,
executive, and judicial. Moreover, he expounded the doctrine of personal as well as functional separation of powers. Emphasizing the personal separation, he declared:
"When the legislative and executive powers are united
in the same person, or in the same body of magistrates,

[27] *Ibid.*, par. xxx, p. 78.
[28] *Ibid.*, par. xxii, pp. 75, 76.
[29] *Of Civil Government*, Bk. II, Ch. XII, pars. 145, 146, 147, p. 191.

there can be no liberty. . . . Again, there is no liberty if the judiciary power be not separated from the legislative and executive." [30] As a matter of fact, however, Montesquieu was not too clear as to the various functions to be found in government and was tempted to accept Locke's classification. "In every government," he observed, "there are three sorts of power: the legislative; the executive in respect to things dependent on the law of nations; and the executive in regard to matters that depend on the civil law." However, in the next paragraph he clarified the above: "By virtue of the first, the prince or magistrate enacts temporary or perpetual laws, and amends or abrogates those that have been already enacted. By the second, he makes peace or war, sends or receives embassies, establishes the public security, and provides against invasions. By the third, he punishes criminals, or determines the disputes that arise between individuals. The latter we shall call the judiciary power, and the other, simply, the executive power of the state." [31] So, although making a distinction in the three departments and pointing out the value of checks and balances, he did not contribute any idea of a constitution which would serve as a source of all governmental power and he did not propose the American concept of coördinate departments.

Montesquieu seems merely to assume the existence of a constitution which grants power "to the body of nobles, and to that which represents the people; each having their assemblies and deliberations apart, each their separate views and interests." He committed the executive power to "a monarch, because this branch of government, hav-

[30] M. de Montesquieu, *Complete Works* (4 vols. T. Evans and W. Davis, London, 1777), Vol. I, Bk. XI, Ch. VI, p. 199.
[31] *Ibid.*, p. 198.

ing need of dispatch, is better administered by one than by many." The judiciary "ought not," he said, "to be given to a standing senate; it should be exercised by persons taken from the body of the people." [32] In discussing the judiciary, he did not rank it on a level with the other two. That he relegated it to a subordinate position is revealed by this statement: "Of the three powers above mentioned, the judiciary is, in some measure, next to nothing: there remain, therefore, only two: and, as these have need of a regulating power to moderate them, the part of the legislative body composed of the nobility is extremely proper for this purpose." [33] Thus, in the end, he accepted the Lockean concept of the departments of government.

Burlamaqui, on the contrary, conceived of the three powers of government, as legislative, executive, and judicial. He did not, however, go into a discussion of the particular departments with the exception of the legislative. Concerning divisions of government, he wrote only incidentally: "For example, if we suppose that the body of the nation reserves to itself the legislative power, and that of creating the principal magistrates; that it gives the king the military and executive powers, etc., and that it trusts to a senate composed of the principal men, the judiciary power, that of laying taxes, etc., it is easily conceived, that this may be executed in different manners, in the choice of which prudence must determine us." [34] He was more specific in the discussion of the powers of sovereignty. He observed that "the first part of sovereignty . . . is the legislative power" and the second is "the coercive power, that is to say, the right of ordaining punishments

[32] *Ibid.*, pp. 200-5.
[33] *Ibid.*, p. 204.
[34] *Politic Law*, Pt. I, Ch. VII, par. xlix, p. 61.

against those who molest the community by their irregu-
larities, and the power of actually inflicting them," and
third that, "it is necessary for the preservation of peace
that the sovereign should have a right to take cognizance
of the different quarrels between the subjects and to decide
them in the last resort . . . this is what we call *jurisdiction*,
or the judiciary power." [35] Clearly they are coördinate;
deriving their respective powers from the same source and
acting independently of each other.

Burlamaqui established the corollary principle of
checks and balances. Locke had no concept of, and indeed
could not have developed, this principle from his idea of
functional separation. Although Montesquieu understood it, he was not as explicit and as emphatic as his con-
temporary, Burlamaqui. Moreover, the chief functions or
departments of government being the legislative and executive, and they not necessarily coördinate, his principle
of checks and balances falls short of the American concept.
"Here, then," Montesquieu said, "is the fundamental
constitution of the government we are treating of. The
legislative body being composed of two parts, they check
one another by the mutual privilege of rejecting. They
are both restrained by the executive power, as the executive is by the legislative." [36]

Explicitly Burlamaqui stated, "this partition produces
a balance of power, which places the different bodies of the
state in such a mutual dependence, as retains every one,
who has a share in the sovereign authority, within the
bounds which the law prescribes to them; by which
means the public liberty is secured. For example, the
regal authority is balanced by the power of the people,

[35] *Ibid.*, Ch. VIII, pars. i-v, pp. 65, 66.
[36] *Works*, Vol. I, Bk. XI, Ch. VI, p. 209.

and a third order serves as a counter balance to the two former, to keep them always in an equilibrium, and hinders the one from subverting the others." [37] Again, in discussing mixed or compound governments, he emphasized the value of limiting the government through a separation of powers and the concurrent limitation of checks and balances. In "mixed or compound governments," he wrote, "it follows, that in all such states, the sovereignty is limited; for as the different branches are not committed to a single person, but lodged in different hands, the power of those, who have a share in the government, is thereby restrained; and as they are thus a check to each other, this produces such a balance of authority as secures the public weal, and the liberty of the individuals." [38]

By means of a highly refined mechanistic structure eighteenth-century liberalism hoped to make safe individual liberty and, simultaneously, to guarantee ultimately the attainment of the common good. The concept of checks and balances fitted into this scheme perfectly. It made possible a relatively greater democracy. On the other hand, it offered a security to those in power against democratic excesses. Burlamaqui gave probably the clearest and most concise theoretical statement of this idea. Yet, his basic thesis of social necessity as a rule for political action would not permit him to accept the present functioning of this power through the Supreme Court.

3

The final concept of American constitutionalism to which Burlamaqui gave a theoretical statement is that of

[37] *Politic Law*, Pt. I, Ch. VII, par. 1, pp. 61, 62.
[38] *Ibid.*, Pt. II, Ch. I, par. xxvi, pp. 76, 77.

an institutional check to the legislature and particularly as a guardian of fundamental law. He did not, apparently, fully develop the idea that the judiciary constituted such an institution, but he, at least, was strongly suggestive of the American idea.

The basis for this further limitation upon the exercise of governmental power he had developed. The constitution was fundamental because it proceeded from the sovereign body politic. It was binding upon all the departments of government. When any department violated its specific grant of power or continued beyond that grant, it was acting without authority and the law was null and void. Enumerating specific limitations which might be imposed by the fundamental law, he concluded that, "indeed the supreme authority is limited in those different respects, insomuch that whatever the king attempts afterwards, contrary to the formal engagement he entered into, shall be void and of no effect." [39]

Pressing the point that government held its power only in trust and that it acted solely within the grant, he asserted: "It is past all doubt that if the sovereign, utterly forgetful of the end for which he was entrusted with the sovereignty, applied it to a quite contrary purpose, and thus became an enemy to the state, the sovereignty returns (*ipso facto*) to the nation, who, in that case, can act towards the person, who was their sovereign, in the manner they think most agreeable to their security and interests." [40]

An editor of Burlamaqui's works included a significant sentence: "When the people, by a body of fundamental law, forbid legislation upon certain subjects, it is evident

[39] *Ibid.*, Pt. I, Ch. VII, par. xlii, p. 57.
[40] *Ibid.*, par. vii, p. 46.

that no legislative proceeding can be had, and no law passed in the country of the kind specified in the constitution." [41] This statement appears in no other edition. In the introduction the editor admitted modernizing the terminology. It is significant that this editor read into Burlamaqui the doctrine of judicial review. All of the teachings of the Swiss jurist lead ultimately to this doctrine.

He did not establish a supreme legislature. The legislative department was "limited in several respects" by the law of nature and by the fundamental law. By acknowledging the former limitation he was following the teachings of Coke and Locke.

Coke, with his idea of the law of nature as a controlling law, issued this dictum in *Dr. Bonham's Case:* "And it appears in our books, that in many cases the common law will control acts of Parliament, and sometimes adjudge them to be utterly void; for when an act is against common right and reason or repugnant, or impossible to be performed, the common law will control it, and adjudge such act to be void." [42] This is the sentence, we are told, the Americans took over and is the germ of judicial review. While it contains the idea, it is also true that, if one looks at the foundation on which it is constructed—reason or the law of nature—it is far from the American constitutional principle. "The statement in the Bonham Case," Mr. MacKay has summarized, "now becomes less formidable, though it still contains the germ of a great idea. It is not an assertion that there is an actual body of law

---

[41] *Principles of Natural and Politic Law* (6th American ed. Riley, Columbus, Ohio, 1859), p. 249.

[42] *Dr. Bonham's Case*, 8 Rep. 118, quoted by MacKay, *loc. cit.*, p. 222.

beyond the authority of Parliament." [43] Coke, however, did provide the institutional check in the courts. They and they alone had the power to determine when parliament violated the fundamental law. Professor Corwin has said of this dictum that as "a form of words . . . , treated apart from his other ideas . . . it became the most important single source of the notion of judicial review." [44]

"The law of Nature," Locke declared, "stands as an eternal rule to all men, legislators as well as others. The rules that they make for other men's actions must, as well as their own and other men's actions, be conformable to the law of Nature . . . and the fundamental law of Nature being the preservation of mankind, no human sanction can be good or valid against it." [45] But he did not provide a means to determine when the legislature had leaped these bounds.

Burlamaqui, reasoning along the same lines as Coke and Locke, limited the legislature by the law of nature. "And as the sovereign holds the legislative power originally of the will of each member of the society," he wrote, "it is evident, that no man can confer on another a right which he has not himself; and consequently the legislative power cannot be extended beyond this limit. Besides, the natural laws dispose of human actions antecedently to the civil laws, and men cannot recede from the authority of the

[43] MacKay, loc. cit., p. 380. However, Corwin, loc. cit., in summarizing Coke's contributions to American constitutional theory said "the doctrine of a law fundamental, binding Parliament and King alike, a law, moreover, embodied to a great extent in a particular document and having a verifiable content in the customary procedure of everyday institutions. . . ."

[44] Corwin, loc. cit., p. 380. Cf. C. G. Haines, The American Doctrine of Judicial Supremacy, Ch. II.

[45] Of Civil Government, Bk. II, Ch. XI, par. 135, p. 185.

former. Therefore, as those primitive laws limit the power
of the sovereign, he can determine nothing so as to bind
the subject contrary to what they either expressly command or forbid." [46]

However, the fundamental law established, he introduced a truly limiting concept of governmental power.
Deriving all power from the constitution, the legislature
was then severely restricted. Another check upon the legislature was effected by dividing it into "different
branches" in such a manner that we may easily see the
extent of their "jurisdiction." [47] The inevitable result of
this line of reasoning is the one to which Burlamaqui arrived; that is, no law can establish an obligation if it proceeds from an improper authority. And when the legislature violates the fundamental law it is acting outside its
authority. Therefore, the law is unconstitutional.

"The authority of the laws," Burlamaqui emphasized,
"consists in the force given them by the person, who, being invested with the legislative power, has a right to enact those laws." [48] The laws enacted by the legislative body
must conform to the fundamental law. The legislature has
no power to enact a law contrary to the constitution for the
legislators are "properly only the executors of the law."
The government was instituted to aid man in the attainment of happiness. When the legislature, a division of
that government, enacts a law contrary to the public security and happiness of the members of the body politic,
the law is of no effect. It is outside the legislative authority. The content of the law must be determined by its
utility. Unless the laws aid the individual, unless the in-

[46] *Politic Law*, Pt. III, Ch. I, par. x, p. 157.
[47] *Ibid.*, Pt. II, Ch. I, par. xx, p. 75.
[48] *Ibid.*, Pt. III, Ch. I, par. xv, p. 158.

dividual derives some benefit or advantage from them, they cannot be said to lay an obligation and they are not, properly speaking, laws. Therefore, in determining the validity of a law its content and source must be considered. In stating the end or purpose of laws, Burlamaqui summarized his position: "We should therefore take care not to imagine that laws are properly made in order to bring men under a yoke. Let us say, rather, that laws are made to oblige the subjects to act according to their real interests, and to chuse the surest and best way to attain the end they are designed for, which is happiness." [49]

The institutional check with which Burlamaqui proposed to protect the fundamental law against the encroachments of the departments of government and as a particular restraint upon the legislature was a "certain assembly" whose consent was essential to the determination of governmental acts. "In a limited monarchy," he affirmed, "there is a certain assembly, who, in conjunction with the king, take cognizance of particular affairs, and whose consent is a necessary condition, without which the king can determine nothing." Or more particularly, "a council, a senate, or parliament" might be established "without whose consent the prince shall be rendered incapable of acting in regard to things which the nation did not think to submit to his will." [50] That it was a judicial body is strongly implied as he proposed at another time that "a senate" be given "the judiciary power." [51]

The germ of the American concept of judicial review is implicit in this sentence: "Thus a parliament, for instance, commanded by the prince to register an edict man-

[49] *Natural Law*, Pt. I, Ch. X, par. iii, p. 99.
[50] *Politic Law*, Pt. I, Ch. VII, pars. xlii, xlv, pp. 58, 59.
[51] *Ibid.*, par. xlix, p. 61.

ifestly unjust, ought certainly to refuse it." [52] Obviously, he was thinking in terms of the French *parlements* which was an institution designed to pass upon and register the edicts of the French monarch. This was an institution especially provided to determine the character and content of law. If the edict of the king was contrary to justice and right reason, it was the duty of the *parlements* to refuse to register it. Burlamaqui, however, conferred upon this body the power of determining the conformity or nonconformity of the statutory law with the fundamental law.

This harmonizes with the earlier American attempts to protect their constitutions. This is demonstrated in the Pennsylvania constitution, 1776, which made provision for a Council of Censors. Also, the New York and Vermont constitutions of 1777 provided for special institutional checks. It is true that these bodies were not required to register laws in the sense of the French *parlements*, yet the functions assigned to them in the respective constitutions were strikingly similar in nature to those performed by that body.

The ease with which the American concept can be read into the works of Burlamaqui is demonstrated by the American edition of 1859. The editor, in publishing this new edition, "modernized" the original translation in this fashion: "Though the people should call for the enactment of such laws, and the legislature pass them, it would be the duty of the courts to declare them null and void, and until the frame of government itself is changed, they would be of no force whatever." [53]

[52] *Ibid.*, Pt. III, Ch. I, par. xxviii, p. 163.
[53] *The Principles of Natural and Politic Law* (Riley, Columbus, Ohio, 1859) p. 249.

The germ of the American concept, though not fully developed, is thus to be found in the teachings of Burlamaqui. With a definite concept of fundamental law and with a limited legislature, he logically introduced the idea of an institution to protect the constitution and to hold the departments of government, particularly the legislature, within the prescribed bounds.

After establishing these numerous controls in a constitutional government he proclaimed the final check—the right of revolution. "But, if the abuse of the legislative power proceeds to excess," he wrote, "and to the subversion of the fundamental principles of the laws of nature, and of the duties which it enjoins, it is certain that, under such circumstances, the subjects are, by the laws of God, not only authorized, but even obliged to refuse obedience to all laws of this kind." [54] Burlamaqui held that the people have only to be convinced that the rulers are planning to oppress them or their rights in order to justify revolution. "Strictly speaking, the subjects are not obliged to wait until the prince has entirely riveted their chains, and till he has put it out of their power to resist him. It is high time to think of their safety, and to take proper measures against their sovereign, when they find that all his actions manifestly tend to oppress them, and that he is marching boldly on to the ruin of the state." [55]

John Adams in the *Novanglus* took this particular paragraph as applicable to the American situation at the outbreak of the American revolution. "Neither are the subjects," wrote Adams, "bound to stay till the prince has entirely finished the chains which he is preparing for

[54] *Politic Law*, Pt. III, Ch. I, par. xviii, p. 159.
[55] *Ibid.*, Pt. II, Ch. VI, par. xxx, p. 130.

them, and put it out of their power to oppose. It is sufficient
that all the advances which he makes are manifestly tend-
ing to their oppression, that he is marching boldly on to
the ruin of the state." [56]

[56] John Adams, *Works* (10 vols. C. F. Adams, ed. Boston, Little and
Brown, 1851), IV, 83.

PART II

BURLAMAQUI AND THE DEVELOPMENT
OF
AMERICAN CONSTITUTIONAL THEORY

4

DISSEMINATION IN AMERICA

A WORK which demonstrated its sustained popularity over a period of a century and a quarter by going through fifty-seven editions in a total of eight countries of the world warrants an intensive study of its content and its influence upon the thinking of the period. A comparatively early printing in America lends much weight to the idea that it was looked upon with favor by the Colonial Americans. Particularly is this latter more probable when the philosophy enunciated in that work so resembles the constitutional theory current in the Colonies, persisting throughout the formative period, and ultimately becoming imbedded in the ground-work of the American constitutional system. After reading Burlamaqui's work, one is curious as to the degree to which he was known to the men in the Colonies before and after the Revolution and, in particular, to the Fathers of the Constitution. Is it possible that this treatise had a direct or indirect relationship to the growth of the characteristically American principles?

It is quite commonplace to reiterate the oft-repeated and always accepted statement that Locke's work was the political bible of the American revolutionists; that the famed Montesquieu was quoted by both high and low to prove salient points; that twenty-five hundred copies of Blackstone's *Commentaries* had been sold before the Declaration of Independence; that Vattel was accepted by all as an authority upon international law; that Grotius, Pufendorf, Hooker, Sydney, Bolingbroke and others less renowned were looked upon with favor. It is not so trite, however, to mention the name Burlamaqui as a source of thought for the Americans from 1760 through the struggle with the mother country and on into the nineteenth century. Indeed, most commentators upon the sources of the ideas of the early American revolutionaries and of the Framers totally ignore or merely mention the name of the Swiss jurist.

It is not the purpose of this work to minimize or to detract from the conventionally accepted influence of these English and Continental authorities. But it is the thesis of the present study that Burlamaqui occupied a position of respect and authority equal, in the main, to any one of the already established and undisputed sources of American ideas and principles. It is its purpose to show (1) that his *Principles of Natural and Politic Law* was present in America; (2) that Burlamaqui was popular during the formative period; (3) and, most important of all, that he was accepted as an authority by those men who are accredited with having the greatest influence upon the formation of the American constitutional system.

In determining the extent of the dissemination and the popularity of the works of Burlamaqui in America during this period, one is forced to look to the public, college and private libraries, to booksellers' lists, auction sales, American editions, and, finally, to the diaries, writings, and letters of the men of the period. Fortunately, there are extant today catalogues from which one may draw a fairly accurate picture of the numerous copies of *Natural and Politic Law* to be found in the Colonies and the States previous to the nineteenth century. In order to appreciate properly the importance which should be attached to the fact that a book could be found upon the shelves of libraries of the eighteenth century, it is well to remember the difficulty under which the men of this period labored in an attempt to secure books; the limited facilities for printing, and the scarcity of public libraries and the limited number of books found in any library. Particularly is this significant when libraries, public and private, large and small, of statesmen, laymen, and ministers from Massachusetts to Georgia contained a specific work. The diaries, letters and writings of the time render a distinct service in determining the content of private libraries. Unfortunately, most of the colleges did not catalogue their collections until approximately 1820. Moreover, many of the libraries did not record the date of accession. Consequently, the approximate date of acquisition is as near as it is now possible to discover.

1

So far as it can be determined from the available evidence, the Library Company of Philadelphia brought the first copy of Burlamaqui's *Natural Law* to America. The accession number shows that the purchase was made before 1757. It is highly probable that this first London edition, 1748, was bought "on the recommendation of the then Librarian, Robert Greenway, of the then Secretary, Benjamin Franklin."[1] A copy of a subsequent London

[1] Letter from the Librarian to the author. This copy carries the accession number 77 O, thus purchased before 1757. *A Catalogue of the Books Belonging to the Library Company of Philadelphia* (1789).

edition, 1752, was purchased by the library before 1770.[2]
The New York Society Library, established in 1754, in
1773 published a partial list of the volumes on its shelves
which included Burlamaqui.[3] A copy of the Dublin edition, 1776, had been added to the collection before 1789.[4]

College libraries acquired copies very early. Before
1764 Harvard College was donated the Geneva edition,
1748, by Thomas Hollis.[5] As shown by the catalogue of
1773 the London edition, 1763, had been purchased
previous to that date.[6] In 1793, the then Librarian of Harvard University, Thaddeus M. Harris, wrote: "Since but
few books can be perused by the generality of people, they
should be those only which are most excellent. The greatest caution is necessary in selecting those of established
reputation from the many that are indifferent or useless."
After this introduction he proceeded to recommend among
others the following: Law, Blackstone and Burlamaqui;
Politics, Montesquieu; Philosophy, Locke's *Essay on Human Understanding.*[7]

[2] Letter from the Librarian to the author. Accession number is evidence
of its purchase before 1770. It is thought that it was acquired about 1760.

[3] *A Catalogue of the Books Belonging to the New York Society Library*
(1773). London edition of 1752 or 1763.

[4] *The Charter, Bye-Laws, and Names of Members of the New York
Society Library with a Catalogue of the Books* (1789); *ibid.*, 1793. Some of
the members: J. J. Astor, Aaron Burr, George Clinton, Thomas Cooper,
De Witt Clinton, Senior Class of Columbia, Philip Freneau, Alexander
Hamilton, R. R., J. R., and W. Livingston. In 1793 appeared the first com-
plete catalogue showing a collection of 5000 volumes.

[5] The seal reads: Ex Dono "Ipsius" Thomas Hollis.

[6] Harvard University, *Catalogus Librorum in Bibliotheca Cantabrigiensi,
selectus, Frequentiorem in usem Harvardinatum, qui gradu Baccalaurei in
artuses* (1773). The succeeding catalogues for 1796, 1798, 1830, and 1840
show additional copies of all new editions.

[7] Thaddeus M. Harris, A.M., *A Selected Catalogue of the Most Esteemed
Publications in the English Language, Proper to form a Social Library with
an Introduction upon the Choice of Books* (1793).

New Jersey College (Princeton) had copies very early. Numerous first London editions which belonged to the College Library and to the Elizabeth Foundation Library are in the Princeton Library. President John Witherspoon introduced Burlamaqui as a text in Princeton in 1768.[8]

The American Circulating Library of Philadelphia [9] and the Union Library of Hatborough, Pennsylvania,[10] contained copies in the Revolutionary period. A copy of the London edition, 1752, was in the Charleston Library Society.[11] The Redwood Library, founded in 1730, acquired a copy of the London edition, 1784, before the books were accessioned.[12]

Burlamaqui's work was being used as a text at William and Mary College in 1779.[13] The following colleges contained copies in the libraries long before 1800: Rhode Island College (Brown University),[14] Dartmouth,[15] and

[8] John Witherspoon, *Lectures on Moral Philosophy* (V. L. Collins, ed., Princeton, Princeton University Press, 1912). Also a letter from V. L. Collins to the author.

[9] *A Catalogue of a Scarce and Valuable Collection of Books at the American Circulating Library of Philadelphia* (1785). William Prichard, editor.

[10] A photostatic copy of *A Colonial Reading List* in the library of the Historical Society of Pennsylvania showing many books withdrawn from the Hatborough Library. A partial list is found in the *Pennsylvania Magazine of History and Biography*, LVI (1932), No. 4. Chester T. Hallenbeck, editor. See also *A Catalogue of Books Belonging to the Union Library of Hatborough* (5th edition, 1847).

[11] *A Catalogue of Books Belonging to the Charleston Library Society* (first catalogue, 1826).

[12] Letter from the Librarian to the author.

[13] All records were destroyed by fire in the middle of the nineteenth century. Dr. E. G. Swem, present librarian, in conversation with the author is confident that Burlamaqui was present on the shelves due to its use as a text and to its wide popularity in Virginia.

[14] *A Catalogue of Books Belonging to the Library of Rhode Island College* (1793); see also *A Catalogue of Books Ordered from England for the Library* (1783). The Library contains some fifteen copies of early editions with no accession numbers.

[15] Foster, *op. cit.*, p. 218. He writes that four copies were acquired before 1796. It was on sale at the "Hanover Bookstore" in 1801.

Columbia.[16] In many of the smaller colleges founded immediately before or just after 1800 the *Principles* may be found in the first catalogues of the libraries: Williams College,[17] Hampden-Sydney,[18] Union College,[19] Dickinson College,[20] Franklin and Marshall,[21] Bowdoin,[22] South Carolina,[23] University of Virginia,[24] Allegheny,[25] Amherst,[26] and the American Literary, Scientific, and Military Academy.[27]

Catalogues of the libraries of many societies which had their beginning before or just after 1800 show numerous copies of the work. For example: The Apprentice's Library Society of Charleston, South Carolina;[28] Linonian, Brothers' and Moral Libraries (Yale College);[29] United Brothers' Society (Brown University);[30] The Mercantile Library of the City of New York;[31] The Union Philosophi-

[16] Possesses numerous early editions.

[17] Letter from the Librarian to the author. Copy of Boston edition, 1792.

[18] Letter from the Librarian to the author. Cambridge edition, 1807.

[19] Letter from the Librarian to the author. Cambridge edition, 1807, two copies.

[20] Letter from the Librarian to the author. Cambridge edition, 1807.

[21] Letter from the Librarian to the author. London edition, 1748.

[22] *A Catalogue of the Library of Bowdoin College* (1821).

[23] *A Catalogue of Books in the South Carolina College Library, August 23, 1814* (1814).

[24] *A Catalogue of Books Belonging to the Library of the University of Virginia* (first catalogue, 1828).

[25] *Catalogus Bibliothicae Collegi Allegheniensis* (1823).

[26] *A Catalogue of the Library of Amherst College* (first catalogue, 1855).

[27] *A Catalogue of the Officers and Cadets of the American Literary, Scientific, and Military Academy* (1822).

[28] *A Catalogue of Books Belonging to the Apprentice's Library Society of Charleston, South Carolina* (1840).

[29] *A Catalogue of Books Belonging to the Linonian, Brothers' and Moral Libraries* (1814).

[30] *A Catalogue of the Library and the Members of the United Brothers' Society* (1853, instituted 1806).

[31] *A Catalogue of the Mercantile Library of the City of New York* (1866).

cal Society;[32] The Philanthropic Literary Society of Hampden-Sydney, Virginia;[33] The Washington Library;[34] The Cincinnati Law Library Association;[35] The Social Friend's and United Fraternity Libraries at Dartmouth College;[36] The Mercantile Library of Baltimore;[37] The Calliopean Society at Yale College;[38] The Main State Library[39] and the Lexington (Kentucky) Library Company.[40]

Burlamaqui's work is listed in the catalogue of the Library of Congress of 1815.[41] A list of the State Department library shows the presence of the Félice edition, 1766, and of a two-volume edition.[42] The Library of Congress has copies formerly belonging to the War Department and the library of the Supreme Court. Two sets were contained in the latter collection.[43] The libraries of the Court of Chancery of New York[44] and the General

[32] Boston edition, 1807, in the Library of Dickinson College.

[33] Letter from the Librarian of Hampden-Sydney College to the author.

[34] *A Catalogue of Books in the Washington, D. C., Library* (1835, inventory of 1834).

[35] *A Catalogue of Law Books Belonging to the Cincinnati Law Library Association* (1852).

[36] Foster, *op. cit.*, p. 218. First catalogue of Social Friend's, 1810, and United Fraternity, 1812. *A Catalogue of Books Belonging to the Social Friends' Library* (1831).

[37] *A Catalogue of the Mercantile Library* (1851).

[38] *A Catalogue of Books Belonging to the Calliopean Society* (1831).

[39] *A Catalogue of Books Contained in the Maine State Library* (1843), prepared by P. C. Johnston, Secretary of State.

[40] *A Catalogue of Books Belonging to the Lexington Library Company* (1821).

[41] *A Catalogue of the Library of Congress* (1815).

[42] *A Catalogue of the Library of the Department of State of the United States, May, 1830.* Félice edition. 8 vols.

[43] Boston edition, 1792; Philadelphia edition, 1823.

[44] *A Catalogue of the Library of the Court of Chancery, April 1, 1842* (Assembly No. 166. Signed by R. Hyde Walworth, Chancellor).

Court of Massachusetts[45] possessed copies. Previous to 1805 the Philadelphia Bar Association purchased a copy of the London edition, 1784.[46]

2

The private libraries of the period attest even more eloquently the esteem with which the works of Burlamaqui were held by the colonists and the Framers of the Constitution. In this connection it is important to remember that the size of private libraries before 1800 seldom exceeded one hundred volumes. In an address to the Bar of Hampshire County, 1826, George Bliss held that in western Massachusetts the largest law libraries contained from fifty to one thousand volumes.[47] In Virginia William Byrd had the largest collection of books numbering 3625 of which 350 were law books.[48]

Probably the first privately owned copy in America belonged to Thomas Hollis of Massachusetts. He purchased numerous books in England in the early fifties of the eighteenth century, some of which he donated to Harvard College. Among those given to the American school was one by Burlamaqui. Incidentally, in addition to his contributions to the library, Hollis founded the chair of philosophy.[49] Delivering an annual election sermon before the Great and General Court of Massachusetts, May 27, 1761, the Reverend Benjamin Stevens, pastor of the First

[45] *A Catalogue of the Library of the General Court of Massachusetts* (1831).
[46] *A Catalogue of the Books Belonging to the Philadelphia Bar Association* (1805).
[47] Charles Warren, *History of the American Bar*, p. 161; see S. L. Knapp, *Biographical Sketches of Eminent Lawyers, Statesmen and Men of Letters.*
[48] Warren, *op. cit.*, p. 162.
[49] A copy of the Geneva edition, 1748, is now in the Harvard Library.

Church in Kittery, quoted at length from Burlamaqui's work. Stevens at that early date referred to Burlamaqui as an "approved writer."[50] Another copy which came to America quite early belonged to President John Witherspoon of New Jersey College (Princeton). This was the Nugent translation, London, 1748. It was probably purchased in England before Witherspoon came to America to take over the duties of the presidency of the College in 1768.[51]

The Election Sermons, delivered within the period 1760 to 1790, evidence conclusively the numerous copies of the Swiss jurist's work within the clergy. Some ministers quote directly, thus leaving no doubt of their contact with the books of Burlamaqui; others mention him by name only; while others show so clearly by the wording, phraseology, and content that one cannot escape the conclusion that they had read or at least had heard expounded his philosophy.[52] Of course, it is impossible to say with absolute accuracy that each of these sermon writers owned a copy of Burlamaqui's work.

A few years after Stevens' sermon quoting Burlamaqui, the Reverend Andrew Eliot, a prominent minister in Boston, preaching to Francis Bernard, Governor of Massachusetts Colony, the Council and the House of Representatives, quoted Burlamaqui extensively.[53] In the pamphlet

[50] Benjamin Stevens, *A Sermon Preached at Boston Before the Great and General Court or Assembly of the Province of the Massachusetts Bay in New England, May 27, 1761* (1761).

[51] Copy in Princeton Library. See William B. Sprague, *Annals of the American Pulpit*, III, 292.

[52] In general, see Alice M. Baldwin, *The New England Clergy and the American Revolution;* and Sprague, *op. cit.*

[53] Andrew Eliot, *A Sermon Preached before His Excellency Francis Bernard, Governor, The Honorable His Majesty's Council, and the Honorable House of Representatives of Massachusetts Bay, May 29, 1765* (1765).

The Crisis, 1766, Reverend Samuel Cooper of Boston depended upon Burlamaqui as an authority for his stand against the power of Parliament to tax the Colonies.[54] Later, in a letter to Thomas Pownall, Governor of Massachusetts, Cooper called Burlamaqui "the eminent Swiss publicist." [55] In 1780 Cooper relied upon him in the first election sermon after the adoption of the new state constitution.[56] The Reverend Timothy Hilliard of Massachusetts, a graduate of Harvard, 1764, owned the London edition, 1784. J. S. Buckminster, a Boston minister, graduate of Yale, 1770, also instructor there, owned a copy.[57] A Reverend Mr. Cary's library, sold at auction in Boston in 1818, contained Burlamaqui.[58] In 1796 Reverend John Clarke, Boston minister, writing letters to a Harvard student, called Burlamaqui one who had done himself "honour in the discussion of moral and political subjects."[59]

Not only the ministers of New England but those of the South were acquainted with the Swiss jurist's writings. Reverend Dr. Samuel Eusebius McCorkle of North Carolina owned a copy very early. Writing of the libraries of the Revolutionary ministers of the South, the Reverend E. W. Caruthers pointed to the fact that in general they were men of small means. They could afford to buy only a few volumes. But in every minister's library certain recog-

[54] Samuel Cooper, *The Crisis, or A Full Defence of the Colonies* (1766).

[55] "Letters from Samuel Cooper to Thomas Pownall, 1769–1777," *American Historical Review*, VIII (January, 1903), 327-28; letter under date of March 25, 1775.

[56] *A Sermon Preached before Governor Hancock, the Senate and the House of Representatives of Massachusetts at the Commencement of the Constitution* (1780).

[57] *A Catalogue of the Library of J. S. Buckminster* (1812), sold at auction.

[58] *A Catalogue of Books, Including the Remains of the Library of the Late Reverend Mr. Cary, Sold at Auction, 1818* (1818).

[59] John Clarke, *Letters to a Student in the University of Cambridge, Massachusetts* (1796).

nized authorities on government and politics could be found. He said that if the minister owned copies of "Pufendorf, Burlamaqui, Montesquieu, and Blackstone, it might be inferred that he was a man who looked below the surface of things."[60]

Burlamaqui's writings were exceedingly popular with the lawyers of this period as one may deduce from the great number who cited or quoted or owned the volumes. Among those familiar with the work were James Otis, 1764;[61] James Wilson in 1770 was quoting it favorably and extensively;[62] Roger Chauncy, a lawyer of New Haven, in 1778;[63] Judge Parker of Portsmouth, 1778.[64] Ephraim Kirby of Litchfield, Connecticut, who studied law with Reynolds Marvin at the close of the Revolution and made the first collection of cases in Connecticut in 1789 known as Kirby's Reports,[65] sold his law books to Seth P. Beers on July 5, 1804, and among them was *Natural and Politic Law*.[66] John Parker Custis, brother-in-law to George Washington and a judge in Virginia, had a copy in 1782.[67] Judge John Tyler of the same state, who

[60] Sprague, *op. cit.*, III, 346; Stephen B. Weeks, "Libraries and Literature in North Carolina in the Eighteenth Century," *Annual Report of the American Historical Association, 1895*, p. 216.

[61] James Otis, *The Rights of the British Colonies Asserted and Proved* (1764), edited by C. F. Mullett as "Some Political Writings of James Otis," *University of Missouri Studies*, IV (July, 1929), 52.

[62] James Wilson, *Considerations on the Nature and Extent of the Legislative Authority of the British Parliament* (1774), in *Works* (2 vols., James De Witt Andrews, editor. Callaghan and Co., Chicago, 1892), II, 507 ff.

[63] Ezra Stiles, *Literary Diary*, II, 35; S. E. Baldwin, "The Study of Elementary Law," *Yale Law Journal*, XIII (October, 1903), 1; Warren, *op. cit.*, p. 181.

[64] Warren, *op. cit.*, p. 181.

[65] *Ibid.*, p. 328.

[66] Dwight C. Kilbourn, *The Bench and Bar of Litchfield County, Connecticut, 1709–1909*, pp. 170 ff.

[67] J. P. Custis, "Catalogue of Library of," *The Tyler Magazine*, IX, 102.

was on the bench of the State Admiralty Court from 1775 to 1788, possessed a copy.[68] Christopher Gore of Boston, in whose office many young men were trained for the law;[69] John Adams;[70] John Quincy Adams;[71] Theophilus Parsons;[72] with whom many studied; George Wythe of Virginia, the intellectual father of a number of noted Virginians;[73] James Bowdoin of Boston, who presided over the State Constitutional Convention, 1779-1780, and was a member of the Massachusetts Ratifying Convention in 1788;[74] James Madison;[75] and Alexander Hamilton[76] were familiar with the name of Burlamaqui. Thomas Jefferson's third library listed a copy.[77] Ezra Stiles, son of the President of Yale, read Burlamaqui's writings in preparation for his law examinations in 1778.[78] Governor J. C. Smith of Connecticut gave the London edition, 1784, to the University of Vermont.[79] Some of the lawyers and judges who became prominent in national affairs after 1800 were also familiar with Burlamaqui, for example: Daniel Webster, who two weeks after graduation wrote,

[68] Letter from President Lyon G. Tyler to the author, March 13, 1933.

[69] Warren, op. cit., p. 186.

[70] Copy of the second edition, London, 1763, in the John Adams collection, now in the Public Library of Boston.

[71] Copy of the three-volume edition at Geneva, 1764, in the Adams Memorial Society Library.

[72] A Catalogue of the Library of Theophilus Parsons Sold at Auction, March 1, 1814 (1814).

[73] Letter from L. G. Tyler to the author, March 13, 1933; E. G. Swem, librarian of William and Mary College; J. S. Reeves, "Influence of Law of Nature upon International Law in the United States," American Journal of International Law, III (July, 1909), 551.

[74] Copy of Boston edition, 1792, Bowdoin College Library.

[75] James Madison, Writings (4 vols., W. C. Rives, ed., Philadelphia, J. B. Lippincott and Co., 1865), I, 613.

[76] Alexander Hamilton, Works (12 vols., H. C. Lodge, ed., New York, G. P. Putnam's Sons, 1904), I, 61; IV, 397, 448.

[77] Copy in library sold to Congress. Geneva, 1756, edition.

[78] Warren, op. cit., p. 181; S. E. Baldwin, The American Judiciary, p. 549.

[79] Letter from the Librarian to the author.

"I next expect to *review* Burlamaqui and Montesquieu";[80] John C. Calhoun,[81] Justice Story,[82] James Kent,[83] and Salmon P. Chase.[84]

Those men who attempted treatises on government around 1800 were quite willing to quote and cite *Natural and Politic Law*, for example Nathaniel Chipman[85] and Thomas Cooper.[86]

To see further the wide dissemination in America of Burlamaqui's works one has only to look at the following list: Reverend Joseph M'Kean, graduate of Harvard, 1794, and professor there in 1806;[87] Joshua Bates, graduate of Harvard, 1800, and president of Middlebury College in 1818;[88] Dr. Cushing Otis, graduate of Harvard, 1789;[89] Samuel Sewell of Boston, graduate of Harvard, 1777;[90] Jeremiah Smith, professor at Harvard;[91] T. Tylston;[92] Witt C. Williams of Virginia;[93] William

[80] Warren *op. cit.*, p. 186. Foster, *op. cit.*, p. 218.

[81] John C. Calhoun, *Works* (R. D. Cralle, ed., New York, D. Appleton & Co., 1854–1856).

[82] Justice Story, *Commentaries on the Constitution of the United States*, (2 vols., Neville M. Bigelow, ed., Boston, Little, Brown and Company, 1891), I, 225.

[83] James Kent, *Commentaries on American Law* (4 vols., C. M. Barnes, ed., Boston, Little, Brown and Company, 1884), Vol. I, Bk I, Lecture I, p. 18.

[84] Foster, *op. cit.*, p. 218.

[85] Nathaniel Chipman, *Sketches of the Principles of Government* (Rutland, Vt., J. Lyon, 1793); *Principles of Government* (Burlington, Vt., Edward Smith, 1833), pp. 12, 22, *supra*.

[86] Thomas Cooper, *Political Essays* (Philadelphia, R. Campbell, 1800).

[87] *A Catalogue of the Select Library of the Late Reverend Joseph M'Kean* (1818), sold at auction. Sprague, *op. cit.*, III, 414.

[88] Copy in Harvard Library; see Sprague, *op. cit.*, II, 465.

[89] Copy of London edition, 1784, in Harvard Library.

[90] *Ibid.*

[91] Copy of London edition, 1784, in Harvard Library. He graduated from Harvard in 1792.

[92] Copy of London edition, 1752 (2 volumes) in Harvard Law Library.

[93] Copy of Dublin edition, 1791; read the work in 1793; letter from Robert C. Hughes, Attorney at Law, Norfolk, Virginia, to the author.

Wirt;[94] N. L. Hooper, graduate of Harvard, 1819;[95] Ebenezer Farley;[96] William Bates of New York;[97] George Bancroft;[98] Nicholas Brown of Rhode Island;[99] Jabez Hammond of New York;[100] Andrew Ritchie;[101] James Breckenridge of Pennsylvania;[102] Ezra Hutchins;[103] Ezekiel Rich;[104] James Stuart;[105] Thomas Storrs;[106] Charles Sumner;[107] Peter C. Brooks;[108] William Clements of Virginia;[109] Gregory Yale, territorial judge in Florida;[110] James Monroe, President of the United States;[111] L. Carberg;[112] Nathaniel Johnston;[113] John Bush;[114] Lewis Jackson;[115] John Logan of Pennsylvania;[116] William Mac-

[94] *A Catalogue of Books Belonging to William Wirt.*

[95] Copy of Cambridge edition, 1807; read it in 1818 in Harvard Law Library.

[96] Copy of Boston edition, 1792, in Harvard University Library.

[97] Copy of London edition, 1784.

[98] *Ibid.,* in American Antiquarian Society Library, Worcester, Massachusetts.

[99] *Ibid.,* in Brown University Library.

[100] Copy in the author's possession.

[101] Copy of London edition, 1784, in Boston Athenaeum.

[102] Copy of Boston edition, 1792, in Library Company of Philadelphia; read in 1827.

[103] *Ibid.,* in American Antiquarian Society Library.

[104] *Ibid.,* in Princeton Library.

[105] *Ibid.,* in New York Public Library.

[106] *Ibid.,* in Massachusetts Historical Society Library.

[107] *Ibid.,* in Harvard University Library.

[108] Copy of London edition, 1752, in Boston Public Library.

[109] *Ibid.,* in Library of Congress.

[110] *Catalogue of the Law Library of Gregory Yale* (1849), sold at auction. London edition, 1752.

[111] Copy of Boston edition, 1792, in Columbia Law Library.

[112] Copy of London edition, 1748, in Library of Congress; read in 1773.

[113] Copy of Lausanne edition, 1783, in Bowdoin College Library.

[114] Copy of London edition, 1748, in Bowdoin College Library.

[115] *Ibid.,* in Library of Congress.

[116] Copy of Lausanne edition, 1783, in Library Company of Philadelphia.

Kinzie of Philadelphia;[117] John Penn, Lieutenant Governor of Pennsylvania;[118] Mr. Priestman;[119] Professor Frisbie;[120] Mr. Field;[121] Joshua Green;[122] I. K. Howe;[123] Sutton Sharpe;[124] and Jasper W. Gilbert, Samuel Miller, and L. Ward Smith, lawyers of Rochester, New York.[125]

The booksellers and auctioneers of the latter eighteenth and early nineteenth centuries advertised for sale copies of Burlamaqui's *Natural and Politic Law*. Some of them were second-hand, others were from private libraries, and others were imported books. The largest and most numerous booksellers of the eighteenth century were to be found in the cities of Boston and Philadelphia, with a few in New York.[126]

[117] William MacKinzie of Philadelphia and a great collector of books. He left his books in 1827 to the Library Company of Philadelphia. He was a great personal friend of George Washington. Letter from the Librarian to the writer. A copy of the *Élémens* (Lausanne, 1784), Library Company of Philadelphia.

[118] John Penn, last of the Penn family to be Lieutenant Governor of Pennsylvania; died in 1795 and left some books to the Library Company of Philadelphia. A copy of *Abrégé du droit naturel* (Genève, 1750), 2 tomes.

[119] *A Catalogue of Books in Mr. Priestman's Library* (1831).

[120] A copy of the Cambridge edition, 1807, in Harvard University Library. Appears to have been used in class in 1819.

[121] A copy of the Cambridge edition, 1807, in Massachusetts Historical Society Library.

[122] A copy of the London edition, 1763, in Harvard Law Library.

[123] A copy of the Cambridge edition, 1807, in Library of Congress. This copy was used by Howe in a class at some university.

[124] A copy of the London edition, 1763, in Harvard Law Library. Mr. Sutton had been a student in Lincoln's Inn.

[125] W. F. Liddle, *Different Libraries in Rochester, New York, on August 31, 1847* (1847), p. 11.

[126] Booksellers and Auctioneers of Boston: John West, W. Hilliard, T. Hilliard, John Boyle, Benjamin Larkin, James White, before 1800; Francis Armory, 1814–1815; Bedlington and Ewer, 1822; and Bond and Company, 1837; Philadelphia: Carey and Lea, 1820; John Grigg, 1830; Washington: George Templeton, 1833; New York: Hugh Gaines, Andrew Barclay, James Inglis, before 1780; T. & J. Swards, Peter A. Nister and James Oram, before 1800.

3

Not only was Burlamaqui popular with the eighteenth-century ministers, laymen, lawyers, and political leaders of both the Tory and the Revolutionary groups, but he was popular with the leading educators of the time both in Europe and in America. No little importance can be attached to the acceptance of Burlamaqui as food for the youth of such universities as Cambridge,[127] Oxford,[128] Paris,[129] Geneva,[130] and Dublin,[131] and particularly for the American young men who attended such colleges as Harvard, Princeton, William and Mary, Columbia, the University of Pennsylvania, Dartmouth, and Brown.[132] Moreover, it is of particular significance that Burlamaqui's works were not an immediate and temporary fancy, but remained in use in many of these colleges far into the nineteenth century. Colleges which had their beginning much later than the above mentioned universities were also attracted to *Natural and Politic Law* as a text; for example, the American Literary, Scientific and Military Academy, now known as Norwich University, Bowdoin College, Maryland University Law School, and the Harvard Law School.

[127] *La Grande Encyclopédie*, VIII, 473; *Bibliographie Universelle*, VI, 195; Adolphie Franck, *Réformateurs et publicistes de l'Europe; moyen age—renaissance*, p. 4; J. J. Burlamaqui, *Principes du droit de la nature et des gens et du droit public général* (Janet et Cotelle, Paris, 1821), "Avertissement de l'éditeur," p. iv.

[128] An edition was published by the Oxford Press, 1817.

[129] An edition published as late as 1850 for the students.

[130] Charles Borgeaud, *Histoire de l'université de Genève*, I, 517.

[131] An edition published in Dublin as late as 1858 with questions for examination by a graduate of the university.

[132] Ernest Nys, *Les États-Unis et le droit des gens*, pp. 143 ff.

Since there were no law schools as such until very late, young men who wished to study law were forced to do so in the office of a lawyer. The first law school was established at Litchfield, Connecticut, by T. Reeves in 1784.[133] Such lawyers as Roger Chauncy of New Haven, Judge Parker of Portsmouth, Theophilus Parsons and Christopher Gore of Boston, James Wilson of Philadelphia, and George Wythe of Virginia took young men into their offices to read law. Each of these lawyers was familiar with the works of Burlamaqui.

It is probably germane to point out the beginning of courses in the field of law and politics in the older American institutions as follows: Harvard, "Ethics and Politicks at Convenient Distances of Time," 1642; King's College, "Ethics and Moral Philosophy," 1762, and "Natural Law," 1773; College of Philadelphia, "Ethics and Moral Philosophy," 1756;[134] New Jersey College (Princeton), "Lectures on Moral Philosophy," 1768; William and Mary College, "Moral Philosophy," and in 1779 the establishment of the first chair of municipal law in the United States. After the reorganization of William and Mary in 1779, the course of Moral Philosophy was taught by Dr. Madison and George Wythe occupied the chair of Municipal Law.[135] Brown University offered a course in "Mathematics and Natural Philosophy," beginning in 1790;[136] Dartmouth College offered "Natural and Politic

[133] James Bradley Thayer, "The Teaching of English Law at Universities," *Harvard Law Review*, IX (1895–1896), 169.

[134] A. Z. Reed, *Training for the Public Profession of Law* (Carnegie Foundation for the Advancement of Teaching, Bulletin No. 15). In general, see Warren, *op. cit.*; William Searle Holdsworth, *Some Lessons from Our Legal History*, Ch. IV; S. E. Baldwin, *The American Judiciary*.

[135] J. F. Colby, "The Collegiate Study of Law," *American Bar Association Reports, 1896*, p. 524.

[136] Warren, *op. cit.*, p. 349.

Law" from 1796 to 1828; in 1790 the University of Pennsylvania instituted a chair of Municipal Law with James Wilson as the first lecturer; and in 1793 King's College secured James Kent to conduct lectures in Municipal Law. The Harvard Law School was opened in 1817, and in the same year the University of Maryland provided for a chair of law with David Hoffman as lecturer.

It is difficult to determine with exactness the texts used in the various colleges in America until well into the nineteenth century. No courses of study were published, but many colleges printed catalogues of students quite early and occasionally included at the end a list of readings required of all students or, at a later date, listed the books required for reading in particular years. Moreover, several students have left a number of books read while in college which gives a fair picture of the education of the period. In addition, there are the catalogues of the college libraries which indicate the books to which the student had access.

Burlamaqui was known for political law rather than for natural and international law. This does not imply that the two latter fields were ignored, but that the colonists and early statesmen looked more frequently to the volume on politic law than to that on natural law. This is further evidenced by the fact that in those catalogues which classified the books Burlamaqui's works are found with Blackstone's *Commentaries* or with Montesquieu and Priestley, while Vattel and Rutherforth were under the heading of international law and Locke under philosophy. This point is emphasized again in noting the order in which the works of these men were given to the students in the colleges. The philosophical works of Locke and Paley were read in the second and third years while Burlamaqui was required for the fourth year usually followed by *The Federalist* and the state constitutions or Vattel. More frequently, Burlamaqui together with the national and state constitutions was the order of study. This is a point of no little significance when one remembers the importance with which Locke's *Two Treatises* were supposedly held throughout this period. When Locke was required reading it was always his *Essay on Human Understanding*.

President Witherspoon of New Jersey College (Princeton) relied extensively upon Burlamaqui in his course, "Lectures on Moral Philosophy," from 1768 to 1775. His Syllabus for this course is extant today and in the list of authorities he included Burlamaqui's *Natural and Politic Law*. Witherspoon's personal copy of the first volume of this work is in the Princeton Library. Upon thumbing through it one finds notes, underlinings, and references made by the owner, indicating no doubt the points of interest to the lecturer. In reading the Syllabus one is struck with the similarity of thought and, in some instances, of wording between Witherspoon and Burlamaqui which, incidentally, correspond with the underlined passages.[137]

Harvard College seems to have used *Natural and Politic Law* as a text quite early. Thomas Hollis, who endowed a chair of philosophy, donated a number of books to the small college library, and among them was Burlamaqui. This copy is preserved in the Harvard library and shows much use, numerous notes and markings throughout. Moreover, the college library acquired before 1773 a copy of the London edition, 1763. It shows much use. In a special catalogue of the library published in 1773 a list of books is given which were most frequently used by all students who received a degree in the arts. It includes Burla-

137 Witherspoon, *op. cit.*

maqui.[138] Furthermore, the Reverend John Clarke in
1796 in advocating the establishment of a chair of politics at Harvard wrote: "The Principles of Natural and
Political Law, by Burlamaqui, have during many
years been studied at the university. . . . His style
is much admired for its clearness and purity; and
the work itself, for uniting, 'after the example of Plato
and Tully, ethicks and jurisprudence, politicks and
religion.' It is the testimony of the translator; and I
have heard the same remark from others, who were thoroughly acquainted with the merits of the performance."
In the closing paragraph Clarke remarked that, so long as
no chair of this type was found there, the students must
read works of recognized authorities "on moral and political subjects. Of this number is Burlamaqui, whose Principles of Natural and Political Law the tutor will explain.
. . . Burlamaqui would lay a foundation for that political
knowledge, which is of infinite importance to a free country." [139] The catalogue of 1798 states that the seniors will
be examined in "Natural and Political Law."[140]

In one of the earliest printed courses of study, as such,
at Harvard in 1818, Burlamaqui was required reading for
the senior class.[141] In the late thirties of the nineteenth century the Harvard Law School published a Syllabus of Law
Studies and under the caption, Introduction and General
Principles; it included Hoffman's *Legal Studies*, volume

[138] *Catalogue Librorum in Bibliotheca Cantabrigiensi, Selectus, Frequentiorem in usem Harvardinatum, qui gradu Baccalaurei in Artuses.*

[139] Clarke, *op. cit.*, Letter No. XII, pp. 109, *et seq.*

[140] *The Laws of Harvard College* (1798).

[141] "Circulating Letter Relating to Harvard University," *North American
Review*, VI (March, 1818), 421. The sophomores read Locke's *Essay on
Human Understanding;* juniors, Paley's *Moral Philosophy;* seniors, Burlamaqui's *Natural and Politic Law.* The class met four days per week the
first semester and five days per week the second.

one of Blackstone's *Commentaries*, volume one of Kent's *Commentaries*, and Burlamaqui's *Natural and Politic Law*.[142] Hoffman recommended very highly the work of Burlamaqui in his *Legal Studies* of 1817 which was published and used as a course of study for the Harvard Law School until 1869.[143] Justice Story wrote a review of Hoffman's book in 1817 in which he described it as "the most perfect system for the study of the law which has ever been offered to the public. The writers whom he recommends are of the very best authority; and . . . we cordially recommend it to all lawyers as a model for the direction of the students who may be committed to their care. . . ." [144]

In the South, Burlamaqui was used quite early in the College of William and Mary. It is definitely known to have been used by George Wythe in his municipal law lectures in 1779. Since there had been a course in moral philosophy for some years preceding, it is thought that it may have been in use much earlier. St. George Tucker, who succeeded George Wythe, was familiar with the work. Mr. E. G. Swem, librarian at the college, states that it was used, no doubt, from 1779 to 1840.[145]

James Wilson, in occupying the newly created chair of Municipal Law in the University of Pennsylvania, 1790, introduced Burlamaqui as a principal source in his lec-

[142] Edmund H. Bennett, *Syllabus of Law Studies*, prepared for Harvard Law School students. No date of publication.

[143] Reed, *op. cit.*, p. 454.

[144] Justice Story, "Review of a Course of Legal Study Respectfully Addressed to the Students of Law in the United States by David Hoffman, 1817," *North American Review*, VI (November, 1817), 75.

[145] Reeves, *loc. cit.*, p. 547; Lyon G. Tyler, *Early Courses and Professors at William and Mary College*, and "A Few Facts from the Records of William and Mary College," *American Historical Association Papers*, IV (October, 1890), 129; letter from Dr. Tyler to the author; conversation with Mr. E. G. Swem, the present librarian, who is an authority on the old public and private libraries of Virginia.

tures. It is not known that he required particular readings, but, it can be stated that, judging from the numerous quotations and citations from *Natural and Politic Law* it was read. These lectures were open to the members of Congress and, at the early lectures, George Washington, the entire Congress, together with the Governor and the Legislature, were in attendance.[146]

In the lectures of James Kent on municipal law at King's College, 1793-1795, Burlamaqui received a place second to none in the quotations and citations in the series. Kent mentions Burlamaqui, also, in his *Commentaries*, 1826.[147]

Dartmouth College, established in 1769, apparently offered no course in law and politics until after the reorganization of the curriculum in 1796. After that date the seniors were provided with lectures in natural and politic law. Since no course of study was published until 1816, one has to presume that the books in use at that date had been the texts since 1796. Professor Colby, in writing of early texts in political science at Dartmouth, said: "Probably the earliest textbooks in each of these subjects were those known to have been in use in 1816. These were the two famous volumes of Burlamaqui's *Principles of Natural and Politic Law*, first published in Geneva in 1747 and republished in Boston as early as 1793."[148] They were pre-

[146] Charles Warren, *History of the Harvard Law School*, I, 172; Wilson, *Works*, I, 40, *et seq.*

[147] James Kent, *An Introductory Lecture to a Course of Law Lectures* (1794); *Dissertations being the preliminary part of a Course of Law Lectures* (1795).

[148] James F. Colby, *Legal and Political Studies in Dartmouth College, 1796-1896*. The date of the Boston edition mentioned by Mr. Colby should be 1792 rather than 1793.

scribed until 1828, when a reorganization in the curriculum was effected.[149]

David Howell, a lawyer of Rhode Island, taught law as well as mathematics and philosophy in Brown University from 1790 to 1824.[150] In the first regular course of study which listed required books, published in 1824, Burlamaqui's works were read by the senior class.[151] Moreover, in the record of books withdrawn from the library for reading during that year, one finds a Mr. Pratt charged with "Burlamaqui, Nat. and Pol. Law (2 vols.)" for Friday October 29, 1824.[152] The library contains numerous copies of early editions of the work which would indicate a popularity at that institution before 1800.[153]

Bowdoin College, Brunswick, Maine, established in 1794, issued the first course of study in February, 1822. It is the opinion of the librarian that the books required in this year had been in use since the opening of the institution. This course of study required Burlamaqui to be read by the seniors in the second semester. The catalogue of 1824 and 1826 contain the same list of required readings. However, the catalogue of 1828 shows a completely new list of readings and some new courses; so it is entirely pos-

---

[149] Foster, *op. cit.*, p. 219. He gives the "Report of the New Hampshire Legislative Committee" of 1816 which lists the texts: Senior year, Locke, *Essay on Human Understanding,* and Burlamaqui's *Natural and Politic Law.* A few years later *The Federalist* was added. *Catalogues of the Officers and Students of Dartmouth College* (1822, 1826, 1827, 1828).

[150] Warren, *History of the American Bar,* p. 349.

[151] *A Catalogue of the Officers and Students of Brown University* (1824).

[152] *Records of Brown University, 1824-1825.* This includes the library record which shows all books withdrawn.

[153] Some of the earlier editions are: Genève, 1747; London, 1784; Genève, 1762; Yverdon, 1766; and Amsterdam, 1751. There are no accession numbers to show when these books were added to the library.

sible that no change had been effected in the course of study previous to 1828.[154]

The American Literary, Scientific and Military Academy, of Norwich, Vermont, also of Middletown, Connecticut, now Norwich University, Northfield, Vermont, established in 1819 and issuing its first course of study in 1822, listed a course in law and politics in which the required reading consisted of "the Constitution of the United States, of the several States, *The Federalist*, Burlamaqui, and Vattel." This course continued unchanged until 1828.[155]

In 1817 when David Hoffman began his lectures at the University of Maryland he published *A Course of Legal Study* in which he put down in outline form a critical survey of the leading authorities in the field of jurisprudence. He recommended highly the *Institutes* of J. J. Burlamaqui in the following words: "This has at all times been a very admired and popular work. . . . The great merit of this production consists in its uniformly ascending to the original principles of the science of morals and politics, and gradually unfolding the subject in a forcible, clear and methodical manner. . . . This little production is very generally placed in the hands of the student; we advise that it should be attentively read."[156] Twenty years later, when

[154] *A Catalogue of the Officers and Students of Bowdoin College, Brunswick, Maine* (1822, 1824, 1826) ; for the first term the senior class read Paley's *Natural Theology*; the junior class read Priestly's *Lectures* and Locke's *Essay on Human Understanding*. Letter from the Librarian to the writer.

[155] *A Catalogue of the Officers and Cadets of the American Literary, Scientific, and Military Academy, Norwich, Vermont;* Prospectus and Internal Regulations of the American Literary, Scientific, and Military Academy to be opened in Middletown, Connecticut, August, 1825; *ibid.*, 1826.

[156] David Hoffman, *A Course of Legal Study Respectfully Addressed to the Students of Law in the United States* (1817), p. 112.

revising this work, he was anxious to have Burlamaqui read by the students.[157] During Hoffman's long tenure as professor of law at the university he published from time to time many of his lectures in which he quoted with approval *Natural and Politic Law*.[158] As has been pointed out, Story wrote a favorable review of the first publication of Hoffman's lectures in 1817. In 1874, R. S. Guernsey said of Hoffman's revised edition : "This is the most valuable and comprehensive work ever published upon the subject to which it relates" and included "the best books."[159]

4

The wide popularity and the wholehearted acceptance of Burlamaqui's works are evidenced again by the comparatively early date of an American edition, to be followed by six editions. The first American printing of *Natural and Politic Law* occurred at Boston in 1792. The demand for this work became so great that Joseph Bustead of Boston agreed to make a reprint of the fourth edition for

---

[157] David Hoffman, *A Course of Legal Study* (2d ed., 1836), I, 112. In this edition he points out that formerly Heineccius, Hutchinson, Cumberland, and Wolf had been used, but he dropped them. Of Burlamaqui and Vattel he said: "We do not hesitate to give a place in our course. . . . We would take occasion here to remark that Burlamaqui's conclusions are not always correct, and he is somewhat tainted with the errors of the Gallic school." He criticized Vattel and recommended only a few chapters of his *Law of Nations.*

[158] David Hoffman, *Syllabus of a Course of Lectures on Law Proposed to be delivered in the University of Maryland* (1821) ; *An Address to Students of Law in the United States* (1824) ; *Legal Outlines: Being the substance of a course of lectures now delivered in the University of Maryland* (1829), I, *et seq.; Introductory Lecture and Syllabus of a Course of Lectures Delivered in the University of Maryland* (1837), Reprint.

[159] R. S. Guernsey, *Legal Bibliography*, p. 4. Also contains the Catalogue of the Library of the New York Law Institute.

three of the booksellers in that city.[160] This was followed
by a second edition printed by W. Hilliard in Cambridge,
Massachusetts, to be sold in his bookstores in Boston, 1807.
It may be argued that 1792 was a rather late date for its
publication in America to affect particularly the American
statesmen of the formative period. However, 1792 was
relatively speaking an early date considering the small
number of books and particularly law books which had
been printed in America. Only thirty-three law books
were published in the Colonies before the Revolution.[161]
William Blackstone's *Commentaries* appeared at Philadelphia in 1771-1772,[162] and the second American edition
was printed at Worcester, Massachusetts, in 1790.[163]
Coke's *Commentaries*, which were quite popular during
this period, did not appear in an American edition before
1800. Emerich de Vattel's *Law of Nations* did not find an
American publisher until 1796.[164] Marten's *Law of Nations* was printed in Philadelphia in 1795.[165] Considering
the writings of Locke and Montesquieu, one is disap-
pointed to learn that Locke's *Two Treatises on Government* passed through only one American printing before
1800.[166] On the other hand, Locke's *Letter Concerning
Toleration* went through three printings before 1800 in
the following order: Wilmington, 1764;[167] Windsor, Ver-

[160] Reeves, *loc. cit.*, p. 551. The booksellers were John Boyle, Marlborough
Street; Benjamin Larkin, Cornhill; and James White, Court Street.

[161] Warren, *History of the American Bar*, p. 157.

[162] Charles Evans, *American Bibliography*, Nos. 11996 and 12327. The
first two volumes in 1771 and the last two in 1772 were printed by Robert
Bell.

[163] *Ibid.*, No. 22265. Isaiah Thomas, Printer. Worcester, Mass.

[164] *Ibid.*, No. 31483, printed by Samuel Campbell, New York.

[165] *Ibid.*, No. 29025, translated by William Cobbett, printed by Thomas
Bradford, Philadelphia, 1795.

[166] *Ibid.*, No. 12834, printed and sold by Edes and Gill, Boston, 1773.

[167] *Ibid.*, No. 9712, printed and sold by James Adams.

mont, 1788;[168] and Stockridge, Massachusetts, 1790.[169] An abridgment of Locke's *Essay on Human Understanding* was printed for the first time in America in 1794.[170] And the first American edition of Montesquieu's *Spirit of the Laws* did not appear until 1800 in Boston to be followed in 1802 by a second and third printing in Worcester and Philadelphia.[171] Burlamaqui's *Natural and Politic Law* passed through a total of seven editions in the United States.[172]

It is apparent, therefore, that Burlamaqui was well known in America before and during the period of the Revolution. His books were imported to this country before 1757. He was cited as early as 1761. In public, college, and private libraries there were copies of his work. He was to be found among the authors in the library of the layman, the minister, the lawyer, the statesman, and the educator. He was to be found not in one area but scattered throughout the Colonies. Booksellers and auctioneers listed his work. It was required reading for all law students, and was used as a textbook by the leading colleges of the period. Finally, there were seven reprintings of his work in the United States from 1792 to 1869. With this wide dissemination in America evidenced, it is next pertinent to inquire into the direct and indirect relation of Burlamaqui's writings to the development of American constitutional theory.

[168] *Ibid.*, No. 21207, printed by Allen Spooner.
[169] *Ibid.*, No. 22622, printed by Loring Andrews.
[170] *Ibid.*, No. 27227, printed by Manning and Loring, Boston, 1794. Abridgment by John Wynne.
[171] Warren, *History of the American Bar*, p. 335.
[172] *Infra,* Appendix II.

5

BURLAMAQUI AND REVOLUTIONARY AMERICA

THE AMERICAN REVOLUTION was a practical application of the theoretical doctrine of the limited state and government. Its philosophical basis asserted the existence of three limits: the purpose of the state, natural law, and popular sovereignty. Of these fundamental concepts the end of the state—the pursuit of happiness—was the most striking innovation in practical political theory. The Declaration of Independence proclaimed to the eighteenth-century world that the pursuit of happiness was a natural, inalienable, and universal right of man. This concept as announced by Jefferson was the consummation and the birth of a long and deeply felt belief. It was the result of the thinking and the experiences of numberless years. It embodied the spirit of the age which was characterized by the cultural, social, and political upheaval of the masses. It was the epitome of the desires of countless nonprivileged individuals for a fuller life the world over.

It is true that the concept of the common good or common weal had been advanced many times. Locke, Priestley, Quesnay, and Hutcheson among others had espoused this idea of state and government.[1] But the two concepts are not to be confused. They are not to be interpreted as being synonymous. To postulate the end of the state in terms of the inalienable right of the pursuit of happiness is far from translating its purpose in terms of the common good.

The latter concept presupposes the attainment of happiness to be a collective right and a social right. It does not advance the idea that the individual happiness is to be considered primary and that the state attains its purpose by seeing that each member is better enabled to gain happiness. Those who advance the idea of the common good postulate the happiness of the individual in terms of the good of society. That which makes for the happiness or general good of society, they argue, must be for the individual good. Therefore, if the individual has a right to happiness it is only a social right. Only as a member of political society may the individual anticipate happiness.

By proclaiming the pursuit of happiness as a natural right the purpose of the state and the functions of government were revolutionized. The new philosophy declared the purpose of the state to be determined by, and through, and because of the personal end of the members composing it. Collective happiness can be measured only in terms of individual happiness. Of necessity the state must be complementary to its members. It converted an otherwise negative theory into a positive theory of the state. In the truly Aristotelian sense the state was regarded as an institution natural to man; natural because it was a means to the ful-

[1] C. M. Wiltse, *The Jeffersonian Tradition in American Democracy*, Ch. IV. Quesnay took from Burlamaqui this idea. See M. E. Daire, *Physiocrates*, pp. 42 ff; also V. L. Parrington, *The Colonial Mind*, p. 344.

fillment of an all-inclusive natural right. It was the antithesis of that theory which presupposed antagonism between
state and individual.

1

As early as 1760 in the struggle between the Colonies
and Great Britain representative colonials were laying the
groundwork upon which Jefferson was to build some sixteen years later. The concept of the pursuit of happiness
was expressed distinctly and boldly, and sometimes, of
course, inadequately and timorously by two groups—the
ministers and lawyers—who furnished the leaders during
the controversy with the mother country. It is significant
that the proponents of this concept, when making acknowledgments, cited Burlamaqui as the source. In contrast,
those who gave Locke as authority made no mention of
happiness as a natural right. Instead, they included property in the list of inalienable rights. Locke specifically
thought that common good was automatically to be pro-
moted by the protection of absolute property rights.

The New England ministers occupied a strategic position in the colonies until the close of the Revolution. They
were the leaders of their respective communities; they
were looked upon as the most learned men of the day; their
opinions were, in the main, the chief source of popular
information until the revolutionary tempo elevated the
lawyers to a place of leadership. They were listened to not
only by their parishioners on the Sabbath but by political
leaders on special occasions such as the annual Election
Sermons and the Artillery Sermons. In the Election Sermons, in particular, the political theory of the ministers
was best expressed. In these instances they were preaching

directly to the Governors and the members of the colonial legislatures. Again, many of the ministers had the opportunity to put into effect their theories of the state and government when serving on committees and as members of state conventions for the drafting and the ratifying of state constitutions as well as the national Constitution.

The prevailing note of the Election Sermons in which Burlamaqui was cited was that of a state limited by the purpose of its creation—the attainment of happiness.

As early as May, 1761, the Reverend Benjamin Stevens, preaching before the Great and General Court of the province of Massachusetts, quoted extensively from Burlamaqui on the subject of civil liberty as being nothing more than natural liberty; that man is made for society and consequently "the supreme law of all governments *is the safety and happiness of the people.*" "Even in absolute monarchies," he paraphrased Burlamaqui, "if the sovereign is influenced by the spirit of Christ and his religion, without any checks to his power or fundamental laws or compact to regulate his conduct, he will make the supreme law of all governments the safety and happiness of the people and not arbitrary will his rule." He held, also, that "civil society is a most salutary institution—a state far best adapted to the happiness of man, according to the present constitution of things."[2]

In the Massachusetts Election Sermon of the following year, 1762, the Reverend Abraham Williams of Sandwich declared man to be fitted for society; that because the "social nature of man, and his natural Desire of Happiness, strongly urge him to Society . . . Civil Societies and governments would be formed; which in this view appear to

[2] *Election Sermon* (1761), Stevens was pastor of the First Church in Kittery.

be natural. To a man detached from Society, many essential parts of his Frame are useless," and thus society is essential.[3]

A prominent Boston clergyman, Andrew Eliot, citing Burlamaqui in 1765, told Governor Francis Bernard and the provincial legislature that man never relinquished natural freedom merely "for the sake of pomp and appearance, much less to gratify the pride and avarice of those over them. The only rational view they can have is the *Common good.*" The measure of the common good was individual happiness. This being the end of the state the government was limited to this purpose.[4]

Dr. Samuel Cooper, whom John Adams described as one of the "most ardent and influential men" of the period and classed with James Otis, Samuel Adams and Peter Thacher, held that the Stamp Act was the use of an arbitrary power "contrary to the principles of equity and reason. The Mother Country had no *just* authority to make an arbitrary law for the taxation of their property."[5] In writing to Thomas Pownall, the liberal Governor of Massachusetts, Cooper criticized the taxing laws of the British Parliament imposed upon the Colonies and cited Burlamaqui, "the eminent Swiss publicist," for the distinction between internal and external obligation to obey law. He conceded that the British Parliament might retain

[3] Abraham Williams, *Election Sermon, May, 1762* (1762). Cf. Burlamaqui, *Natural Law*, Pt. I, Ch. IV, par. iii, p. 37: "Hence we observe a natural inclination in mankind that draws them toward each other and establishes a commerce of services and benevolence between them, from whence results the common good of the whole, and particular advantage of individuals."

[4] *Election Sermon* (1765), pp. 8, 22. "Wisdom and knowledge are very necessary qualifications of a public ruler." Cf. Burlamaqui, *Politic Law*, Pt. I, Ch. VII, pars. xviii, xix, pp. 50-51. Also see note above.

[5] *The Crisis*, p. 2; John Adams, *Works*, IX, 284.

some "external *Obligations*" but it had "lost the internal Obligation."[6]

The Reverend Daniel Shute, in the Massachusetts Election Sermon, 1768, agreed with Burlamaqui that "civil government among mankind is not a resignation of their natural privileges, but that method of securing them, to which they are morally obliged as conducive to their happiness." And when the rulers have subverted the end or the purpose of its creation the individual is "obliged to resist them."[7]

Dr. John Tucker of Newbury preached to Thomas Hutchinson, 1771, that "civil government is founded in the very nature of man, as a social being, and in the nature and constitution of things. . . . It is manifestly for the good of society." The purpose of the state must be the attainment of individual happiness.[8] Likewise, the Reverend Samuel Lockwood was preaching to the General Assembly of Connecticut, 1774, that man was intended naturally for society; that it was through society he gained the most happiness by gratifying his social virtues and that the end of the state is "general security and public happiness." The end constituted a limit to the power of the rulers which secured the rights of the people.[9]

Illustrative of those who relied upon Locke in their Election Sermons is Stephen Johnson who, in preaching to the General Assembly of the Colony of Connecticut,

[6] "Letters of Samuel Cooper to Thomas Pownall, 1769–1777," *American Historical Review*, VIII (January, 1903), 327-28. Letter of March 25, 1773.
[7] *Election Sermon* (1768), pp. 21, 41 ff. Cf. Burlamaqui, *Natural Law*, Pt. II, Ch. VI, par. ii, p. 191. "Government is so far from subverting this first order that it has been rather established in order to give it a new degree of force and consistency."
[8] *Election Sermon* (1771), pp. 12, 13, 19 *et seq.*
[9] *Election Sermon* (1774), p. 7.

1770, said: "Important are the rights of mankind, to the safe and unmolested enjoyment of life, liberty and property, and to the best improvement of all their powers, with every reasonable and equitable advantage they have to promote their present and everlasting welfare. These natural rights, civil and religious, are the gifts of God, as such sacred; nor may any but He, as original proprietor, resume them at pleasure. But in such a world as this, lying in wickedness, abounding with unruly passions, mistaken views, clashing interests and violence, there can be no rational foundation for the security of them, without civil government."[10]

On the eve of the writing of the Declaration of Independence, Samuel West declared the law of nature to be a perfect law and concluded: "This shows that the end and design of civil government cannot be to deprive men of their liberty, or take away their freedom; but on the contrary the true design of civil government is to protect men in the enjoyment of liberty. From hence it follows that tyranny and arbitrary power are utterly inconsistent with, and subversive of the very end and design of civil government, and directly contrary to natural law. . . . Whenever they act contrary to the end and design of their institution, they forfeit their authority to govern the people. . . . Consequently the authority of a tyrant is of itself null and void."[11]

[10] *Election Sermon* (1770), p. 1. See also *Election Sermons* of Edward Door (1765), Gad Hitchcock (1774), Edward Bernard (1766).

[11] *Election Sermon* (1776), p. 14. Cf. Burlamaqui, *Politic Law*, Pt. I, Ch. VII, par. xix, p. 51. "It must therefore be acknowledged, that it never was the intention of the people to confer absolute sovereignty upon a prince, but with this express condition, that the public good should be the supreme law to direct him; consequently so long as the prince acts with this view, he is authorized by the people; but, on the contrary, if he makes use of his power merely to ruin and destroy his subjects, he acts intirely of his own head, and not in virtue of the power with which he was entrusted by the people."

Likewise, the lawyers, who assumed control of the public mind after 1765, conceded the purpose of political society to be the attainment of happiness. At this early date James Otis was the pronounced exponent of the doctrine of the law of nature. He was a student of the Continental natural law philosophers. It is highly doubtful that he was unfamiliar with the writings of Burlamaqui. According to John Adams, Otis had read the *Principles of Natural and Politic Law* along with the works of Pufendorf, Grotius, Barbeyrac and Vattel.[12] He criticized the writings of Pufendorf and Grotius because they only "state facts, and the opinion of others" from which nothing can be deduced.[13]

The passage of the Revenue Act, 1764, occasioned the writing of *The Rights of the British Colonies Asserted and Proved*. The political philosophy of James Otis is to be found in this, his most popular writing and in the opinion of Professor Wright probably the most influential tract until Dickinson's *Farmer's Letters*. One of the two principles he enunciated in this pamphlet is that the state and government are natural to man and must be justified by their purpose; or, as John Adams characterized this point, "those laws should have no other end ultimately but the good of the people."[14]

"Government is founded *immediately* on the necessities of human nature," Otis wrote, "and *ultimately* on the will of God, the author of nature; who has not left it to men in general to choose, whether they will be members of society or not, but at the hazard of their sense if not of their

[12] *Works*, IX, 275; see C. F. Mullett, *Fundamental Law and the American Revolution*, p. 32.

[13] Mullett, "Some Political Writings of James Otis," *University of Missouri Studies*, IV (July, 1929), p. 65. Otis also cited Montesquieu, Locke, Coke, Harrington and Heineccius.

[14] *Works*, X, 293.

lives. Government having been proved to be necessary by
the laws of nature, it makes no difference in the thing to
call it from a certain period *civil*."[15] Had not Burlamaqui
insisted, in contrast to Locke and the Mediaevalists, that
the political state was the true natural state of man?[16]
Moreover, Otis, like Burlamaqui, was not particularly concerned with the immediate origin but let it be "placed
where it may, the *end* of it is manifestly the good of *the
whole*." The nature of the state is determined by the end
and "the *end* of government, being the *good* of mankind,
points out its great duties." Thus, the state, to Otis, was
positive in character because of the "duties" which it assumed to the individuals. But, at the same time, the state
is not unlimited for "there is no one act which a government can have a *right* to make that does not end to the advancement of the security, tranquility and prosperity of
the people."[17]

Likewise, James Wilson a few years later was to pro-
claim a broad philosophical basis for political authority.
Although trained in the law he had a thorough understanding of and respect for the principles of political philosophy underlying legal arguments. He enthusiastically
accepted the writings of Burlamaqui. Probably he cited
and quoted the works to a greater extent than any American. Not only is Burlamaqui present in his writings but
also in his debates in the Convention. Indeed, it can be

[15] Mullett, "Some Political Writings of James Otis," *University of Missouri Studies*, IV (July, 1929), p. 54.

[16] *Politic Law*, Pt. I, Ch. III, par. xiii, p. 15. "Let us therefore examine
into natural and civil liberty; let us afterwards endeavour to shew, that
civil liberty is far preferable to that of nature, and consequently, that the
state which it produces, is of all human conditions the most perfect, and,
to speak with exactness, the true natural state of man."

[17] Mullett, "Some Political Writings of James Otis," *University of
Missouri Studies*, IV (July, 1929), 53, 55 ff.

safely said that the philosophy of James Wilson was essentially that of Burlamaqui. Constantly he was citing and
quoting the Swiss jurist in the *Considerations on the Nature and Extent of the Legislative Authority of the British
Parliament* written in 1770 and published four years
later.

Wilson accepted the primary thesis of Burlamaqui that
individual happiness is the ultimate goal of political society. He maintained happiness to be a natural right.
Political society was introduced only "to ensure and to
increase the happiness of the governed above what they
could enjoy in an independent and unconnected state of
nature. The consequence is that the happiness of the society is the first law of every government."[18] He then
quoted from Burlamaqui that "the right of sovereignty is
that of commanding finally—but in order to procure real
felicity; for if this end is not obtained, sovereignty ceases
to be a legitimate authority." That the power of the state
is determined by its purpose is a rule, Wilson contended,
"founded on the law of nature; it must control every political maxim : it must regulate the legislature itself." [19]

To Wilson political society was the natural and inevitable growth of man. There were no basic differences between the natural and political states of man. With
approval he quoted Burlamaqui that civil society is nothing

[18] *Works*, II, 507. Cf. Burlamaqui, *Politic Law*, Pt. I, Ch. V, par. vi, p. 32:
"I add, in fine, to procure their own happiness, etc., in order to point out
the end of sovereignty, that is, the welfare of the people."

[19] *Works*, II, 508. Wilson quoted Burlamaqui as follows: "When sovereigns lose sight of this end, when they pervert it to their private interests,
or caprices, sovereignty then degenerates into tyranny, and ceases to be
legitimate." Cf. Burlamaqui, *Politic Law*, Pt. III, Ch. I, par. x, p. 157:
"Therefore, as those primitive laws limit the power of the sovereign, he can
determine nothing so as to bind the subject contrary to what they either
expressly command or forbid."

more than natural society perfected. Upon this statement Wilson commented that " 'Tis for the security and improvement of such a state that the adventitious one of civil government has been instituted." Man being naturally a social creature, therefore "to a state of society we are invited from every quarter. It is natural; it is necessary; it is pleasing; it is profitable to us. The result of all this is that for a state of society we are designed by Him, who is all-wise and all-good." [20]

Alexander Hamilton, in his *Farmer Refuted*, 1775, admonished his adversary in the *Westchester Farmer* to apply himself "without delay to the study of the law of nature. I would recommend to your perusal Grotius, Pufendorf, Locke, Montesquieu, and Burlamaqui." Hamilton quoted freely from Burlamaqui in *Pacificus*. In a letter to George Washington, 1793, he described him as "an approved writer." [21]

In considering the relation of the colonies to Great Britain with regard to the extent of subordination, Hamilton held that this "must be ascertained by the spirit of the constitution of the mother country, by the compacts for the purpose of colonizing, and, more especially, by the law of nature, and that *supreme law* of every society—*its own happiness*." [22] But the colonies had no sanctions against the British parliament. And, Hamilton continued, since "we are without those checks upon the representatives of Great Britain which alone can make them answer the end of their appointment to us; which is the preservation of

[20] *Works*, I, 255.
[21] Hamilton, *Works*, I, 62; IV, 397, 448.
[22] *Ibid.*, I, 66. Cf. Burlamaqui, *Politic Law*, Pt. I, Ch. VII, par. xix, p. 51. "That it was not the intention of the people to confer absolute sovereignty upon a prince but with this express condition, that the public good should be the supreme law to direct him."

the rights, and the advancement of the happiness of the governed, the direct and inevitable consequence is, *they have no right to govern us.*"[23]

Moreover, paraphrasing Burlamaqui, Hamilton contended that "the fundamental source of all your errors, sophisms, and false reasonings is a total ignorance of the natural rights of mankind. Were you once to become acquainted with these, you could never entertain a thought that all men are not, by nature, entitled to a parity of privileges. You would be convinced that natural liberty is a gift of the beneficent Creator, to the whole human race and that civil liberty is founded on that and cannot be wrested from any people without the most manifest violation of justice. *Civil liberty is only natural liberty, modified and secured by the sanctions of civil society.* It is not a thing, in its own nature, precarious and dependent on human will and caprice; but it is conformable to the constitution of man, as well as necessary to the *well being* of society. . . . For, if it be conducive to the happiness of society (and reason and experience testify that it is), it is evident that every society, of whatsoever kind, has an absolute and perfect right to it, which can never be withheld without cruelty and injustice."[24]

In the same year John Adams expressed the same idea. There is evidence that he had read this concept in Bur-

[23] *Works*, I, 68. Cf. Burlamaqui, *Politic Law*, Pt. I, Ch. VII, par. xviii, p. 51. "The civil state must necessarily empower the subjects to insist upon the sovereign's using his authority for their advantage, and according to the purpose for which he was entrusted with it."

[24] *Works*, I, 69. Hamilton's italics. Burlamaqui, *Politic Law*, Ch. III, par. xxv, p. 19. "Civil liberty . . . is natural liberty itself, divested of that part which constituted the independence of individuals by the authority which it confers on sovereigns." In par. xxi, he wrote that "the civil state . . . is far more perfect, more secure, and better adapted to procure his happiness than that which he was possessed of in the state of nature."

lamaqui. Although he did not cite him until the turn of the century, one has the distinct impression that he was embodying many of Burlamaqui's ideas before the outbreak of the Revolution. Adams owned the second London edition, 1763, of *Natural and Politic Law*. These volumes, now in the John Adams Collection in the Boston Public Library, show much use and many interlineated and notated passages. It is significant that these particular passages correspond with his expressed ideas.

Adams, in a letter to George Wythe, 1775, stated as the paramount principle of government its ultimate purpose —happiness. "We ought to consider what is the end of government," he wrote, "before we determine which is the best form. Upon this point all speculative politicians will agree, that the happiness of society is the end of government, as all divine and moral philosophers will agree that the happiness of the individual is the end of man. From this principle it will follow that the form of government which communicates ease, comfort, security or, in one word, happiness, to the greatest number of persons, and in the greatest degree, is the best."[25]

In his copy of *Politic Law* Adams marked the following passages: "It is certainly one of the most important questions in politics, and has most exercised the men of genius to determine *the best form of government*."[26] Again, "That government ought to be accounted the most complete which best answers the end of its institution and is attended with fewest inconveniences."[27] And again he marked the paragraph in which Burlamaqui wrote of the magistrates making "use of their authority, pursuant to

[25] *Works*, IV, 193.
[26] Burlamaqui, *Politic Law*, Pt. II, Ch. II, par. i, p. 82.
[27] *Ibid.*, par. iii, p. 83.

the views and purposes for which they were intrusted with it, and agreeably to the intention of the Deity, that is, for the happiness of the people."[28]

Adams categorically denied the hypothesis of Montesquieu that political authority is founded upon fear. "Fear, which is said by Montesquieu and other political writers, to be the foundation of governments, is so sordid and brutal a passion that it cannot possibly be called a principle."[29] Furthermore, he had reason to criticize some of the teachings of Locke and others. "Americans in this age," Adams wrote, "are too enlightened to be bubbled out of their liberties, even by such mighty names as Locke, Milton, Turgot, or Hume; they know that popular elections of one essential branch of the legislature, frequently repeated, are the only possible means of forming a free constitution, or of preserving their lives, liberties, or properties in security; they know, though Locke and Milton did not, that when popular elections are given up, liberty and free government must be given up."[30]

The basic principle of happiness as a natural right, which had gained such wide-spread acceptance among the leaders during the controversial period previous to the actual political break with the mother country, became in the Declaration of Independence a practical principle of government underlying the American concept of state and government. In the second paragraph of this document Jefferson summarized and crystallized the theoretical and practical thinking of the time. "We hold these truths to be self-evident," it declares, "that all men are created equal, that they are endowed by their Creator

[28] *Ibid.*, Pt. I, Ch. VI, par. xi, p. 40.
[29] *Works*, IV, 203.
[30] *Ibid.*, p. 466.

with certain unalienable Rights, that among these are Life, Liberty and the Pursuit of Happiness. That to secure these rights, Governments are instituted among Men, deriving their just powers from the consent of the governed. That whenever any Form of Government becomes destructive of these ends, it is the right of the people to alter or abolish it, and to institute a new Government, laying its foundation on such principles and organizing its powers in such form, as to them shall seem most likely to effect their safety and Happiness."

The long controversy that has been waged as to Jefferson's sources has been adequately treated by Professor Carl Becker.[31] He demonstrated the close similarity of the above quoted paragraph with a passage from James Wilson's *Considerations*. In addition, Professor Chinard has discovered that Jefferson in his *Commonplace Book* copied extensively from this pamphlet. However, Jefferson did not insert the paragraph bearing the most striking resemblance: "All men are, by nature, equal and free: No one has a right to any authority over another without his consent: All lawful government is founded on the consent of those who are subject to it: Such consent was given with a view to ensure and to increase the happiness of the governed above what they could enjoy in an independent and unconnected state of nature. The consequence is that the happiness of the society is the first law of every government."[32]

Professor Chinard manifestly, and correctly, had the opinion that Jefferson was not dependent upon Locke or Montesquieu. He has suggested that Lord Kames may have recommended the idea to Jefferson. It is true, too,

[31] *The Declaration of Independence.*
[32] Wilson, *Works*, II, 507. See Gilbert Chinard, *Thomas Jefferson*, p. 73.

that Jefferson had copied extensively from Kames' *Historical Law* in his *Commonplace Book*. The suggestive idea of one of these passages is the contention by Kames that natural rights, which may have included the right to happiness, were not altered after entering into political society. "Mutual defence," wrote Kames, "against a more powerful neighbor being in early times the chief, or sole motive for joining in society, individuals never thought of surrendering any of their natural rights which could be retained consistently with their great aim of mutual defence."[33]

In the underlying political philosophy of the Declaration of Independence, Jefferson and Locke are at two opposite poles. The inalienable rights of man as enumerated by Locke were life, liberty and property. According to Jefferson they were life, liberty and the pursuit of happiness. The substitution of the phrase pursuit of happiness for property was revolutionary in character. And Jefferson properly understood all its implications. It was no mere rhetorical or euphonic flourish on the part of Jefferson. This was the very core of his philosophy. To have admitted property as a natural right and consequently as a foundation of the state would have been contrary to his very nature. This is demonstrated in the letters which passed between Jefferson and Du Pont de Nemours.[34] The omission of the inalienable right of property was a conscious and intentional act. This has been irrefutably demonstrated by Professor Chinard. Among the Jefferson papers is a copy of Lafayette's draft of the *Déclaration des*

[33] Chinard, *op. cit.*, p. 84. "Such a philosophy of natural rights had never before been expressed by any political philosopher, I have been able to refer to, with one possible exception."

[34] Gilbert Chinard, *The Correspondence of Jefferson and Du Pont de Nemours.*

droits de l'homme et du citoyen. In listing the natural rights Lafayette had included *le droit à la propriété.* Jefferson upon reading the paper placed in brackets this phrase. This suggests its deletion and, what is more significant, the elimination of property as a natural right of man.[35]

This very important concept of natural rights is further substantiated by a paper in the Jefferson Collection written by Thomas Paine. It is highly probable that they had discussed the problem before the writing of the passage. It embodies the earlier thinking of Jefferson. After its publication in Paine's *Rights of Man,* Jefferson, in a letter to Monroe, admitted that he "professed the same principles."[36] The passage deals with the reasoning and subsequent activity of a number of individuals who move into an uninhabited region. "It would then occur to them," it reads, "that their condition would be much improved if a way could be devised to exchange that quantity of danger into so much protection so that each individual should possess the strength of the whole number. As all their rights, in the first place, are natural rights and in the exercise of those rights, supported only by their own natural individual power, they would begin by distinguishing between those rights they could individually exercise fully and perfectly and those they could not.

"Of the first kind are the rights of thinking, speaking, forming and giving opinions, and perhaps all those which can be fully exercised by the individual without the aid of exterior assistance—or in other words, rights of personal competency. Of the second kind are those of personal

[35] Chinard, *Thomas Jefferson,* p. 84. See also Chinard's *Letters of Lafayette and Jefferson,* p. 82. See also V. Marcaggi, *Les origines de la déclaration des droits de l'homme de 1789,* pp. 111-24. Burlamaqui is considered as one of the chief sources.

[36] *Writings* (20 vols., Memorial Edition, Washington, 1907), VIII, 207.

protection of acquiring and possessing property, in the exercise of which the individual natural power is less than the natural right."[37]

Paine's division of rights into natural and acquired is similar to that of Burlamaqui. The listing of property under the heading of the latter type is both Burlamaquian and Jeffersonian. It seems to be quite impossible to determine any direct acquaintance which Paine may have had with Burlamaqui's works. The striking resemblance of this passage with one from the latter's *Natural Law* may be demonstrated. "Rights are natural and acquired. The former are such as appertain originally and essentially to man, such as are inherent in nature and which he enjoys as man, independent of any particular act on his side. Acquired rights . . . are those which he does not naturally enjoy, but are oweing to his own procurement."[38] Moreover, he had declared, earlier in his treatise, that property was an acquired right. It was one of the "adventitious" states of man.[39] Excepting the rather vague statement by Lord Kames, Burlamaqui was the only recognized authority who had advanced an idea similar to that of Paine and Jefferson.

Burlamaqui as one source for the phrase, "pursuit of happiness," and its underlying philosophy rests upon a number of factors. Jefferson owned a copy of *Natural and Politic Law*. It is conceded that George Wythe, with whom Jefferson studied law, was familiar with the work. In all

[37] Chinard, *Thomas Jefferson*, p. 81. Professor Chinard originally assigned this statement to Jefferson, but corrected it in his *Correspondence of Jefferson and Du Pont de Nemours*, p. lxxiii. It is found in Paine's *Rights of Man* (London, J. Jordan, 1791), pp. 44-45, and in M. D. Conway, *The Life of Thomas Paine*, I, 235. Conway believes that it was written about 1788.

[38] *Natural Law*, Pt. I, Ch. VII, par. vi, p. 71.

[39] *Ibid.*, Ch. IV, par. vi, p. 40.

probability Dr. Small, one of Jefferson's mentors, was acquainted with it. In reading and copying Wilson's pamphlet he imbibed freely the doctrine of Burlamaqui. Moreover, the concept was a rather common one in the thought of the period. The similarity of the concept with that of Burlamaqui is unmistakable. This has been noted by Fisher in his study of this period.[40] Professor Corwin declares a striking likeness. However, he is of the opinion that the immediate source of the phrase was Blackstone.[41] If this should have been the case, it came originally from Burlamaqui. In the early portion of the *Commentaries* Blackstone copied liberally from *Natural and Politic Law*. Sir Henry Maine has charged that Blackstone copied "textually" from Burlamaqui.[42] Again, granting that Jefferson took the idea from Wilson's *Considerations*, it must be remembered that Wilson copied and cited Burlamaqui as an authority for the concept. Upon the evidence at hand it is submitted that the original of the phrase "pursuit of happiness" is *Natural and Politic Law*.

The concept of the state as expressed in the Declaration of Independence continued in the thought of the period for another decade. However, it was fighting a losing battle with the antithetic concept of property as an inalienable right. This transition in the thinking of the Americans between 1776 and 1787 is a study within itself. It has not been done adequately.

The conservative revolt of this decade demonstrated the real nature of the Revolution. It was not basically a social

---

[40] Sydney George Fisher, *The Struggle for American Independence*, I, 462.

[41] Corwin, *loc. cit.*, p. 402. He cites Blackstone's *Commentaries*, I, 41, and Locke, *Of Civil Government*, Bk. II, Ch. XIX, par. 225.

[42] Sir Henry Maine, *Ancient Law*, p. 114. See Reeves, *loc. cit.*, pp. 547 *et seq.*

revolution as the Declaration of Independence had proclaimed and as many of the people, particularly the lower
classes, had been led to believe. With the return of order
the people began to look forward hopefully and to demand
the practical redemption of the promised socially revolutionary doctrine. But it was not forthcoming. For the most
part, the struggle between the two major economic divisions—creditor and debtor—took the form of legal and
peaceful methods; yet, from the viewpoint of the creditor
class, very effective and highly destructive. The emergence of the concept of property as a natural right and
its inclusion in the Constitution as a basic foundation of
the new system proceeded from the democratic excesses,
as described by the creditor class, during this period. Some
of the Legislatures had fallen into the hands of the debtor
class. The result was the passage of inflationary laws
which struck a vulnerable and vital spot in the creditor
class. After describing the financial condition of the national government, the historian Von Holst writes that
"the pecuniary condition of the individual states was still
worse, for here there was not only no possibility of pay-
ment, but the disposition to pay became weaker every day.
And even when existing legislatures could be reproached
with nothing on this score, it was so uncertain what might
be expected from future ones that the state scrip could be
negotiated only at an oppressive premium. And this became continually worse, for the number of those who
aimed at liquidating their debts by a dishonorable exercise
of the legislative power constantly increased, and in many
states it became more uncertain every day whether they
could not find a majority in the legislature." [43] But cheap
money was not condoned by the creditor class.

[43] H. Von Holst, *The Constitutional and Political History of the United States*, I, 41.

These legislatures, however, did not stop here. They passed stay laws, thus granting immediate relief to the debtor and just as immediately and effectively striking at the creditor. Shays' Rebellion was merely another manifestation of the social conflict between the propertied and the nonpropertied classes. Von Holst in his account charges that "the malcontents who either openly or secretly sided with Shay were equal in number to the friends of the state government, and their ultimate object was none other than the repudiation of public and private debts and a redistribution of property."[44]

The outlook was ominous. If property were not immediately installed as a sacred right it might be too late. It is noteworthy that following the demonstration of force on the part of those who had placed their hope and confidence in the practical application of the socially revolutionary doctrine of the Declaration, immediate efforts were made to secure a Constitution in order to strengthen the position of the creditor class. One of Mr. Randolph's speeches on the Convention floor summarizes the opinion of the majority of that body. It demonstrates clearly the anti-democratic feeling in that gathering. "One idea has pervaded all [our] proceedings, to wit, that opposition as well from the States as from individuals, will be made to the System to be proposed. Will it not then be highly imprudent, to furnish any unnecessary pretext by the mode of ratifying it? Added to other objections agst. a ratifica-

---

[44] *Ibid.*, p. 45. See A. C. McLaughlin, *Confederation and the Constitution, 1783–1789*, p. 142. "But the argument of the needy or shiftless," writes McLaughlin, "was easy: the property of the United States had been protected from destruction by the joint exertion of all, it ought therefore to be the common property of all. The man that opposed this creed was declared to be 'an enemy to equality and justice,' who should 'be swept from the face of the earth.' " In Charles C. Thach's *The Creation of the Presidency*, may be found the most complete study.

tion by Legislative authority only, it may be remarked that there have been instances in which the authority of the Common law has been set up in particular States agst. that of the Confederation which has had no higher sanction than legislative ratification. Whose opposition will be most likely to be cited agst. the System? That of the local demagogues who will be degraded by it from the importance they now hold. These will spare no efforts to impede that progress in the popular mind which will be necessary to the adoption of the plan, and which every member will find to have taken place in his own, if he will compare his present opinions with those brought with him into the Convention. It is of great importance therefore that the consideration of this subject should be transferred from the Legislatures where this class of men have their full influence to a field in which their efforts can be less mischievous."[45]

Yet there were a few who dared to assert their faith in the doctrine of the Declaration and in the teachings of Burlamaqui. Representatives of this group follow.

The Model Constitution for Massachusetts drafted by John Adams in 1779 gives a prominent place to the teachings of the Declaration of Independence. Of course, this is a restatement of his position in 1775. Or it may have been a paraphrasing of the Declaration itself. "The end of the institution, maintenance, and administration of government is," the preamble reads, "to secure the existence of the body politic; to protect it, and to furnish the individuals who compose it with the power of enjoying, in safety and tranquillity, their natural rights and the blessings of life, and wherever these great objects are not obtained, the people have a right to alter the government,

[45] *Records of the Federal Convention of 1787*, (Max Farrand, ed.), II, 89.

and to take measures necessary for their safety, happiness, and prosperity." Article I, Chapter I declares that "all men are born free and *independent*, and have certain natural, essential and unalienable rights . . . in fine, that of seeking and obtaining their safety and happiness."[46]

In the Pennsylvania ratifying convention, 1787, James Wilson restated his earlier position when he observed that "Civil government is necessary to the perfection of society. We now remark that civil liberty is necessary to the perfection of civil government. Civil liberty is natural liberty itself, divested only of that part which, placed in the government, produces more good and happiness in the community." And, again, when delivering his lectures at the University of Pennsylvania, 1790, he declared: "How often has the end been sacrificed to the means! Government was instituted for the happiness of society; how often has the happiness of society been offered as a victim to the idol of government. Let government—let even the constitutions be, as they ought to be, the handmaids; let them not be, for they ought not be, the mistress of the state."[47]

Because the members of the Constitutional Convention had violated their instructions and the amending procedure of the Articles of Confederation in preparing the Constitution and in putting it into effect, James Madison felt the necessity of a justification of these acts. In defense he offered the theory of natural rights; particularly the important right to the pursuit of happiness. In doing this he was relying upon the socially revolutionary doctrine

---

[46] Adams, *Works*, IV, 219-20.

[47] *Works*, I, 538 and 271. He was paraphrasing Burlamaqui, *Politic Law*, Pt. I, Ch. III, pars. xiii, xiv, pp. 18, 19. This is exceptionally good counsel in 1937.

of 1776 and Burlamaqui to justify the establishment of a system of government which refused to pay homage to that philosophy. "They must have reflected," he wrote, "that, in all great changes of established governments, forms ought to give way to substance; that a rigid adherence in such cases to the former would render nominal and nugatory the transcendent and precious right of the people to 'abolish or alter their governments as to them shall seem most likely to affect their safety and happiness.' They must have recollected that it was by this irregular and assumed privilege, of proposing to the people plans for their safety and happiness, that the States were first united against the danger with which they were threatened by their ancient government. . . . The sum of what has been here advanced and proved is . . . that if they had exceeded their powers they were not only warranted, but required . . . by the circumstances in which they were placed to exercise the liberty which they assumed; and that, finally, if they had violated both their powers and their obligations in proposing a constitution, this ought, nevertheless, to be embraced, if it be calculated to accomplish the views and happiness of the people of America." [48]

Citing Burlamaqui frequently, James Kent, in his law lectures at Columbia University, 1795, defined the state as "the union of free individuals by common consent to promote their safety and happiness." Citing Burlamaqui and Barbeyrac as authorities, Kent said that man was "fitted and intended by the great Author of his being for society and civil government." Furthermore, he observed

[48] *The Federalist* (H. C. Lodge, ed. New York, G. P. Putnam's Sons, 1889), No. 39. See Witherspoon, *op. cit.*, pp. 70-72. Burlamaqui was a reading in this course.

that Burlamaqui, "a modern writer" belonged to the school of thought of Aristotle and Plato.[49]

The first attempt at a systematic study of government in the United States was the *Sketches of the Principles of Government* by Nathaniel Chipman in 1793. In this work Chipman relied upon Burlamaqui for a number of principles. Criticizing those philosophers who held that the state was not in keeping with the nature of man and that only in the state of nature did "virtue and happiness" flourish, he observed that "a more careful investigation of the subject can but show us that man is, by the laws of his nature, fitted for a state of society." Recent revolutions, however, "have, by degrees, opened the eyes of all mankind. They have, in some instances, learnt, and have even dared to assert, that all legitimate government is founded in the rights of the people; that it is an institution for their convenience and happiness; that the ruler has no right as a man, beyond that of every individual; and that his power, which he exercises, is not his power but the power and right of the people, entrusted for their benefit."[50]

2

There was no concept more pronounced in the formative period of American constitutionalism than that of popular sovereignty. Sovereignty resided originally and always in the people. The body politic, the result of a social compact, was the reservoir of all political power. Sovereignty, however, was always something less than the

[49] *Dissertations Being the Preliminary Part of a Course of Law Lectures in Columbia University*, pp. 5, 10.
[50] Pp. 31, 50, 105.

absolute; it could not be arbitrary. It could not be identified with the sheer essence of absoluteness. The political philosophy underlying the American Revolution was a practical contradiction of the concept of the state as possessed of unlimited power. Always, it was limited by natural law and its purpose. The Americans, upon the basis of their interpretation of popular sovereignty, demanded more than a theoretically limited government. They required the imposition of checks, specifically established, in order better to safeguard individual liberty.

It is not maintained that Burlamaqui was the chief source of this concept. He cannot be ignored, however, as a contributing factor in its crystallization. It had been a cardinal principle of the Americans throughout the seventeenth and eighteenth centuries. Roger Williams and John Davenport had been outspoken exponents of the doctrine very early. The doctrine of popular sovereignty could have been gleaned from many sources as well as from the experiences of the Americans themselves. It was common property. The peculiarly American application of it, however, is strikingly similar to that of Burlamaqui.

A representative statement of the source of political power, so far as the politically minded ministers were concerned, was that of Andrew Eliot, who, citing Burlamaqui, declared that "all power has its foundation in compact and mutual consent, or else it proceeds from fraud and violence."[51] Or, as Benjamin Stevens observed, "but tho' civil power is the ordinance of heaven, yet it is to be considered as granted by the people." The most immediate source of sovereignty was the consent of the whole of the individuals.[52] Daniel Shute caustically observed that the

[51] *Election Sermon* (1765), p. 17.
[52] *Election Sermon* (1761), p. 54.

only right which individuals had to authority over other men was by the consent of the whole, and that, indeed, "this delegation is not the giving away of the right the whole have to govern, but providing for the exercise of their power in the most effectual manner."[53]

In 1764 James Otis in expressing the current American thought stated explicitly the concept of Burlamaqui. "It [sovereignty] is therefore *originally* and *ultimately* in the people. I say supreme absolute power is *originally* and *ultimately* in the people; and they never did in fact *freely*, nor can they *rightfully* make an absolute, unlimited renunciation of this divine right. It is ever in the nature of the thing given in *trust*, and on a condition, the performance of which no mortal can dispense with; namely, that the person or persons on whom the sovereignty is confer'd by the people, shall incessantly consult *their* good."[54] Regarding the method of delegation, he held that "the form of government is by *nature* and by right so far left to the *individuals* of each society that they may alter it from a simple democracy or government of all over all to any other form they please. Such alteration may and ought to be made by express compact; But how seldom this right has been asserted history will abundantly show."[55]

James Wilson, second only to Madison in his influence on the formation of the Constitution, 1787, probably had the clearest insight into the theory of constitutional government and the principle of popular sovereignty. Wilson

[53] *Election Sermon* (1768), p. 22.

[54] Mullett, "Some Political Writings of James Otis," *University of Missouri Studies*, IV (July, 1929), 52. Cf. Burlamaqui, *Politic Law*, Pt. I, Ch. VII, par. xxvi, p. 53.

[55] Mullett, "Some Political Writings of James Otis," *University of Missouri Studies*, IV (July, 1929), 54.

did not understand nor did he suggest the sovereignty of the State. The only sovereignty of which he admitted was that of the whole people. Moreover, the sovereignty of the body politic was not unlimited. Its purpose automatically restricted its power. "When the society was formed," he wrote, "it possessed jointly all the previously separate and independent powers and rights of the individuals who formed it, and all the other powers and rights which result from the social union. The aggregate of the powers and these rights composes the sovereignty of the society or nation. In the society or nation this sovereignty originally exists."[56]

Wilson took the very sentences and phrases of Burlamaqui in explaining the establishment of political power. "In order to constitute a state," he wrote, "it is indispensably necessary that the wills and the powers of all the members be united in such a manner that they shall never act nor desire but one and the same thing, in whatever relates to the end, for which the society is established. It is from this union of wills and of strength that the state or body politic results. The only rational and natural method, therefore, of constituting a civil society is by the convention or consent of the members who compose it. . . . The union is a benefit, not a sacrifice: Civil is an addition to natural order."[57]

In his "Consideration on the Bank of North America,"

---

[56] *Works*, I, 166-69.

[57] *Ibid.*, p. 272. Cf. Burlamaqui, *Politic Law*, Pt. I, Ch. IV, pars. iv, v, p. 23. "It was necessary to unite forever the wills of all the members of the society, in such a manner, that from that time forward they should never desire but one and the same thing in whatever relates to the end and purpose of society. . . . It is from this union of wills and of strength, that the body politic or state results, and without it we could never conceive a civil society."

1785, Wilson had occasion to point out that the Confederation was not intended to transfer or abridge any rights "to which the United States were previously entitled. . . . It is no new position that rights may be vested in a political body which did not previously reside in any or in all the members of that body. They may be derived solely from the unison of those members. 'The case,' says the celebrated Burlamaqui, 'is here very near the same as in that of several voices collected together, which, by their unison, produce a harmony, that was not to be found separately in each.' " [58]

John Adams, also, asserted the basis of all political power to be the consent of the people. Passages which Adams marked in his copy of Burlamaqui resemble very closely the content of some of his statements concerning the situs of sovereignty. For example, in his *Defence of the Constitution,* Adams observed that "sovereignty resides in the whole body of the people . . . and can reside nowhere else." [59] And in the Model Constitution one reads that "all power residing originally in the people, and being derived from them, the several magistrates and officers of government, vested with authority, whether legislative, executive, or judicial, are their substitutes and agents, and are at all times accountable to them." [60] The reason for the contractual basis of society was to insure

[58] Wilson, *Works* (3 vols. Bird Wilson, ed. Philadelphia, Lorenzo Press, 1804), III, 407. He cited Burlamaqui, *Politic Law*, pp. 41-42.

[59] *Works*, IV, 270.

[60] *Ibid.*, p. 220. Cf. Burlamaqui, *Politic Law*, Pt. I, Ch. V, par. vi, p. 39. "It must therefore be agreed that sovereignty resides originally in the people and in each individual with regard to himself." Like Burlamaqui, Adams followed with the example of Rome. See *Politic Law*, Pt. II, Ch. I, par. xxii, p. 75, "They, who thus share the sovereignty among them, are properly no more than the executors of the law, since it is from the law itself that they hold their power."

the attainment of the "common good."[61] In light of his earlier statements, Adams was not here using "common good" as synonymous with the "general good." Likewise, Hamilton, in 1775, was defending the doctrine of consent as the only basis of legitimate government. "The origin of all civil government, justly established," he wrote, "must be a voluntary compact between the rulers and the ruled and must be liable to such limitations as are necessary for the security of the *absolute rights* of the latter; for what original title can a man, or set of men, have to govern others, except their own consent?"[62]

3

The third concept assumed by the Declaration of Independence was a higher law, a law superior to all human law, a law emanating from human nature or right reason, which was obliging upon man and upon the state and government, namely, a law of nature. The law of nature was a perfect law which, if obeyed, inevitably led to the attainment of the good life or happiness. It guaranteed to the individual certain inherent rights. "It is in this conception of the law of nature," Professor J. A. Smith has written, "as guaranteeing certain rights to the individual and limiting governmental authority, that we find the principle which largely determined the character of the early constitutional development of the United States."[63]

Burlamaqui, considered solely as an exponent of natural rights, does not differ materially from other represen-

[61] Adams, *Works*, IV, p. 219.

[62] *Works*, I, 63.

[63] J. Allen Smith, *The Growth and Decadence of Constitutional Government*, p. 12.

tatives of the natural rights school. His chief contribution
does not lie, however, in his interpretation of natural law
as a body of principles limiting both state and government; a limitation which required no explicit constitutional expression to be valid. Rather, it is to be found in
the idea of a written document which further limited the
government.

It is true, however, that Burlamaqui's influence in what
may be called the field of natural law proper was not in-
considerable. This has been demonstrated so clearly that
it needs no further elucidation. Professor B. F. Wright
notes that Burlamaqui, along with Pufendorf, constituted
the most important continental source and, though "practically unknown at the present time, it was one of the
most popular of political treatises among the Americans
in the second half of the eighteenth century."[64] Dean
Roscoe Pound has observed that the early Americans were
faced with the problem of giving "certain fundamental
concrete content to natural rights at once and at the out-
set. We did this by taking our philosophical mold from
Grotius and Pufendorf and Vattel and Burlamaqui, and
pouring into that mold a concrete content from Coke's
Second Institute and Blackstone's *Commentaries*."[65] Professor Jesse S. Reeves has written that frequent references
were made to Burlamaqui "who treated the law of nature
in its broader sense."[66] In the opinion of C. G. Haines,
Burlamaqui was one of the representative authorities on

[64] B. F. Wright Jr., *American Interpretations of Natural Law*, pp. 7, 8,
44, 85, 89, 281.

[65] Roscoe Pound, "The Theory of Judicial Decision," *Harvard Law
Review*, XXXVI (May, 1923), 804.

[66] Reeves, *op. cit.*, pp. 547 ff.; also his "La Communaute Internationale,"
Académie de Droit International, *Recueil des Cours*, 1924, II, 33.

natural law in the formative period of American constitutional development.[67]

Specifically in regard to the idea of a "higher law" Professor E. S. Corwin has noted the relationship of Burlamaqui to this particular American concept.[68] Moreover, Professor C. F. Mullett has demonstrated that Burlamaqui was a source of this idea and arrived at the conclusion that "in any case, while Locke was quoted with much frequency, the actual number of references to his name, if one wished to be statistical, did not greatly, if at all, surpass those of certain others, notably Coke and Burlamaqui."[69]

The well-known fact that the course of the dispute with Great Britain led the colonists from arguments based on the British constitution to wider ones relative to the rights of man probably impressed the significance of Burlamaqui's distinction between a "higher law" and the constitution. Typical of such arguments are the following expressions.

In 1765 Edward Door, preaching to the Assembly of Connecticut, charged that "as rulers of this people, you are bound, by a law superior to any human constitutions."[70] Two years later the Reverend Ebenezer Bridge told the Massachusetts Legislature that all laws enacted "must be . . . consistent with those laws which had an existence prior to the existence of the state, and those upon which the state was founded, if rightly founded, or else

[67] C. G. Haines, *The Revival of Natural Law Concepts*, p. 50.
[68] Corwin, *op. cit.*, pp. 42, 149, 402 *et seq.*
[69] Mullett, *Fundamental Law and the American Revolution, 1760-1776*, pp. 78, 30, 32, 189.
[70] *Election Sermon* (1765), p. 22.

the constitution will be receded from and altered."[71] And Jason Haven, 1769, distinguished clearly between the sources of the respective rights of man. "Rulers," he said, "should not only be acquainted with the natural rights of the people, which are the same under every form of government, but also with those which originate from the constitution of the country where they live."[72] Another minister disciple of Burlamaqui, Andrew Eliot, 1765, declared to Governor Francis Bernard that "whatever form of civil government we have chose, there are certain constitutions, which are the basis and foundation of the state, and which are obligatory on those who govern, as well as those who are governed."[73]

The concept of two fundamental laws was the general reasoning of the period. Experience over a period of years played its part in determining this concept. But the Americans were wont especially to cite an authority. For this idea they found Burlamaqui adequate. James Otis, 1764, popularized this basic principle of subsequent American constitutional theory. "The same law of nature and reason is equally obligatory on a *democracy*, an *aristocracy*, and a *monarchy:* Whenever the administrators, in any of those forms, deviate from truth, justice, and equity, they verge towards tyranny and are to be opposed." And, in the oft-quoted passage, his position is more clearly stated. "Parliaments are in all cases to *declare* what is for the good of the whole; but it is not the *declaration* of parliament that makes it so. There must be in every instance a higher authority, viz., God. Should an act of Parliament be against any of *his* natural laws, which are *immutably*

[71] *Election Sermon* (1767), p. 19.
[72] *Election Sermon* (1769), pp. 26, 40.
[73] *Election Sermon* (1765), p. 19.

true, *their* declaration would be contrary to eternal truth, equity and justice and, consequently, void; and so it would be adjudged by the Parliament itself, when convinced of their mistake."[74]

James Wilson, likewise, distinguished clearly between the fundamental law of nature and the fundamental constitution. In doing so he accepted explicitly the teachings of Burlamaqui. The law of nature, Wilson held, "must control every political maxim : It must regulate the legislature itself." The constitution established additional limitations upon the rulers and, where provisions are expressly made and limitations set by laws, "his government shall be conducted according to those limitations . . . that in no case shall it be conducted contrary to the express or to the implied principles of the constitution."[75] And Alexander Hamilton declared that "the laws of nature and the British constitution both confine allegiance to the person of the king, and found it upon the principle of protection."[76]

James Madison called upon the higher law—the law of nature—in defense of the adoption of the new constitution. "Two questions of a very delicate nature present themselves on this occasion," he wrote, "1. On what principle can the Confederation, which stands in the solemn form of a compact among the States, be superseded without the unanimous consent of the parties to it? . . . The first question is answered at once by recurring to the absolute necessity of the case. To the great principle of self-preservation, to the transcendent law of nature and of

[74] Mullett, "Some Political Writings of James Otis," *University of Missouri Studies,* IV (July, 1929), 55, 70.

[75] *Works* (Andrews, ed.), II, 508, 558. Cf. R. G. Adams, *Political Ideas of the American Revolution,* pp. 136-41.

[76] *Works,* II, 61.

nature's God, which declares that the safety and happiness of society are the objects at which all political institutions aim, and to which all such institutions must be sacrificed."[77]

[77] *The Federalist*, No. 52, quoted in Smith, *op. cit.* p. 120. See also Madison, *Writings*, I, 613; Nys, *op. cit.*, pp. 59-60.

6

BURLAMAQUI AND AMERICAN
CONSTITUTIONAL GOVERNMENT

By 1787 the Americans had evolved a rather complete theory of constitutional government. Theoretically it was based upon the three concepts dealt with in the last chapter. One notable exception must be indicated. The Constitution has lent itself to an interpretation which has exalted property rights to a place of primary importance and submerged the pursuit of happiness doctrine. However, there is a Burlamaquian tradition in American constitutional theory. It has lain dormant for decades only to come to life and terrify those who would extinguish it. Basically, the American system rests upon the theory proclaimed by Burlamaqui in 1747 and accepted by Jefferson in 1776. That system envisioned by Jefferson was not hide-bound. It was a living, growing constitution. Social necessity was the maxim of those two men. The supreme function of the state was to make possible the realization of happiness.

Although submerged for long periods of time, the progressive theory of the Declaration experienced revivification in the administrations of Jefferson, Jackson and Wilson. But it is under the New Deal that the theory has had its greatest and most aggressive resurgence. Mr. Roosevelt has aimed consciously at the giving of a new life to this theory. He has attempted to give it a real meaning in the national life. When he proclaims "the more abundant life," he is redeeming the philosophy of the Declaration of Independence.

The system established in 1787 proceeded from the assumption that all political power is limited and, further, that its exercise by government be specifically curbed by the application of certain principles. The source of these principles is difficult to determine. But the most complete theoretical statement of the system is to be found in Burlamaqui. The striking similarity of his teachings to the American development of constitutional government is undeniable. For three basic concepts of that system Burlamaqui was a direct or indirect source: the constitution as a fundamental law, the system of checks and balances based upon coördinate departments, and, finally, judicial review.

The Americans were not misled by the teachings of Locke, Montesquieu, Coke, and others to a belief that the only fundamental law necessary was the law of nature. Rather, they were definitely convinced that a law emanating from the sovereign body politic in the form of a covenant or a constitution was necessary further to restrict government. This conclusion was the result of the basic idea that all sovereignty, though not in the sense of legal omnipotence, resided in the people. The American people gave a practical application to the theoretic teaching of Burlamaqui that the fundamental law was an additional check upon government.

1

It is not maintained that Burlamaqui was the only authority upon whom they relied for this concept. The American concept of a constitution as a fundamental law had its historical background, as Professor McLaughlin has so well shown, in the covenants of the Church, in the early charters, and in the corporate trading companies.[1] Through experience this concept had become a part of the thinking of the men of the constitution-making period, 1776–1787. But the leaders were not content to rest their case upon their experiences alone. They appreciated the teachings of theorists which substantiated their position. The leaders of this period were familiar with virtually the only complete theoretical statement of this principle —Burlamaqui. Not only had many of them read him, but others had no doubt received instruction in Burlamaqui's *Politic Law* in the leading universities of the colonies between 1765 and 1780. Moreover, the ministers preaching before the colonial legislatures constantly restated the position that a constitution is fundamental and the source of all governmental power. It is more than a mere coincidence that those ministers who are known to have been familiar with the writings of Burlamaqui stated this concept in unequivocal terms. To them the constitution was a means through which the people made secure the powers of government. In short, it was to them a special precaution taken by the people to insure limited government.

[1] *The Foundations of American Constitutionalism*, Chs. I, II, III. Vattel, incidentally, mentioned the fundamental character of a constitution. It should be pointed out that he studied under Burlamaqui at the University of Geneva.

Benjamin Stevens quoted Burlamaqui to the effect that the authority conferred by the people upon the sovereign must be "attended with a right of insisting on his making a good use of this authority, and with a moral security that this right will have its effect."[2] Andrew Eliot, likewise, declared that "when government is founded in mutual consent, it is the undoubted right of the community to say who shall govern them, and to make what limitations or conditions they think proper."[3] Samuel Cooper, who had actively opposed the work of the Massachusetts Assembly in 1778,[4] preached the annual election sermon in 1780 commemorating the new government. "Unhappy the people," he declared, "who have not the ulterior powers of government within themselves . . . and who at the same time have no fixed constitutional barrier to restrain this reigning power." Near the close of the sermon he exclaimed: "Happy people! Who . . . have deliberately framed the constitution under which you chuse to live, and are to be subject to no laws, by which you do not consent to bind yourselves."[5]

Again, John Tucker, a Boston minister, stressed the fact that only "authority derived from the community and granted by them can be justly exercised, only within certain limits, and to a certain extent, according to agreement. . . . The very being and form of government, with all its constitutional laws, being theirs from the people, hence civil government, is called, and with great propriety, the *ordinance of men—an human institution.*" Specifically, the constitution, he held, was "properly, the su-

---

[2] *Election Sermon* (1761), p. 9.
[3] *Election Sermon* (1765), p. 18.
[4] Alice M. Baldwin, *op. cit.*, p. 137.
[5] *Election Sermon* (1780), pp. 15, 26.

preme power, being obligatory on the whole community
—on the highest officer as well as the lowest subject."[6]

The Reverend Charles Turner demanded a constitution to control governmental authority. "Rulers are so
prone to have vastly at heart certain worldly interests, inconsistent with the publick welfare, and the duty they owe
the community that it is incumbent on the people . . . to
fix on certain regulations, which if we please we may call
a *Constitution*, as the standing measure of the proceedings
of government, so determining what powers they will invest their rulers with, and what privileges they will retain
in their own hands."[7]

This basic concept of American constitutionalism—
i.e., that the fundamental law sets up restrictions in addition to the law of nature—which had been nurtured by
the ministers was taken over by the political leaders.
Here, too, one finds acknowledgments to Burlamaqui. In
many instances when no direct citation is made the connection is very suggestive.

In the Provincial Convention of Pennsylvania, 1775,
James Wilson explained the nature and purpose of the
British constitution. "Of this great compact between the
king and the people, one essential article to be found on his
part is that, in those cases where provisions are expressly
made and limitations set by laws, his government shall be
conducted according to those provisions and restrained according to those limitations. . . . It shall be conducted . . .
to their ultimate end—the interest and happiness of his

[6] *Election Sermon* (1771), pp. 16, 29.

[7] *Election Sermon* (1775), p. 16. Cf. Burlamaqui, *Politic Law*, Pt. I, Ch.
VII, par. xxxv, p. 55. "It entirely depends upon a free people to invest the
sovereigns . . . with an authority . . . limited by certain laws. . . . These
regulations, by which the supreme authority is kept within bounds, are
called *the fundamental laws of the state*."

subjects—that in no case shall it be conducted contrary to the express, or to the implied, principles of the Constitution."[8]

Very early Wilson summarized the American concept of fundamental law as the following paragraph demonstrates. "By the term constitution I mean that supreme law, made or ratified by those in whom the sovereign power resides, which prescribes the manner according to which the state wills that the government should be instituted and administered. From this constitution the government derives its power, and by this constitution the power of the government must be directed and controlled; of this constitution no alteration can be made by the government because such alteration would destroy the foundation of its own authority."[9] In the Pennsylvania ratifying convention, 1787, he emphasized again the source of fundamental law by declaring that "as our constitution is superior to our legislatures, so the people are superior to our constitutions."[10] Although making no reference to any authority, it should be noted that immediately preceding this statement he had taken without acknowledgment an entire paragraph from Burlamaqui. Finally, he declared in his lectures on law at the University of Pennsylvania that the one important contribution of the United States to "political science" was the written constitution as a supreme law "made and ratified by those in whom the sovereign power of the state resides."[11]

John Adams, in 1775, contended that the British Parliament had no authority to alter the fundamental Ameri-

[8] *Works*, (Andrews, ed.), II, 588.
[9] *Ibid.*, I, 417.
[10] *Ibid.*, p. 543.
[11] *Ibid.*, p. 352.

can law. The basis of this contention was purely legal in nature. It was not a question of utility but one of constitutional theory. The source of all power being in the body politic and the constitution emanating from that sovereign body, that a legislature could change the fundamental law was contrary to his basic principle. "The question we insist on most is," he wrote, "not whether the alteration is for the better or not, but whether parliament has any right to make any alteration at all. And it is the universal sense of America that it has none."[12] It is significant that Adams underlined, in his personal copy of Burlamaqui, the following: "The constitution . . . can be changed only in the same manner, and by the same methods, by which it was established, that is to say, by the unanimous concurrence of all the contracting parties."[13]

The Model Constitution, of which Adams was the author, emphasized the point that the convention had the power to draft a constitution, but that it could not take effect until the people approved it. In Article V one reads: "All power residing originally in the people, and being derived from them, the several magistrates and officers of government, vested with authority, whether legislative, executive, or judicial, are their substitutes and agents, and are at all times accountable to them."[14] Adams underscored the following passage from Burlamaqui: "They, who thus share the sovereignty among them, are properly no more than the executors of the law, since it is from the law itself that they hold their power."[15]

The General Court of Massachusetts, elected under the

[12] *Works*, IV, 120.
[13] *Politic Law*, Pt. II, Ch. I, par. xxiv, p. 76.
[14] Adams, *Works*, IV, 220, 224.
[15] *Politic Law*, Pt. II, Ch. I, par. xxii, p. 75.

colonial charter, assumed the power to draft a constitution for the State. Concord, among other towns, objected to this procedure. The Concord Town Meeting demanded that a constitutional convention be called for this specific purpose. The report of this Town Meeting was drawn up by a committee consisting of "two or three farmers, the village cordwainer, and a Harvard M.A." The resolutions were presented to the General Court, October 22, 1776. They state succinctly the subsequent procedure in making American constitutions. "That the Supreme Legislative, either in their proper capacity or in joint committee, are by no means a body proper to form and establish a constitution or form of government, for reasons following. First, because we conceive that a Constitution in its proper idea intends a system of principles established to secure the subjects in the possession and enjoyment of their rights and privileges, against any encroachments of the governing part. Second, because the same body that forms a constitution has of consequence power to alter it. Third, because a Constitution alterable by the Supreme Legislative is no security at all to the subject against any encroachment of the governing part on any or on all of their rights and privileges."[16] Obviously, this committee was not following the teachings of Locke. That which they were protesting against—the supreme legislature—was the core of Locke's constitutionalism.

The conformity of Thomas Jefferson to Burlamaqui's teachings has been noted. Particularly was this evident in the Declaration of Independence. Also, the striking similarity between them and with Tom Paine respecting the concept of rights has been evidenced. It is in this respect

[16] S. E. Morison, ed., *Sources and Documents of the American Revolution, 1774-1786*, p. 176.

that Jefferson added, as did Burlamaqui, a principle which was essential to the establishment of the concept of the constitution as a fundamental law. It has been observed that Jefferson, in drawing the distinction between natural and acquired rights, was not following Locke. Professor Chinard believes this may be accounted for in Jefferson by his legal training. "The theory of the social compact," writes Chinard, "may have come from Locke; certainly it did not come from Rousseau; but Jefferson introduced into it a fundamental modification when he distinguished between real natural rights and the civil rights guaranteed by society but limited in order to provide for more safety. At any rate, Jefferson's conception of the social compact was far more rigorous, precise and specific than any that had been proposed before. A man who had been trained as a lawyer knew exactly what a contract was, and how necessary it is, in such an instrument, to write clauses safely guarding both parties."[17]

Jefferson, in his *Notes on Virginia*, deplored the condition existing in that state whereby the legislature was superior to the constitution. The ills which had befallen the Virginia government, he declared, could be laid to the manner of adopting the fundamental law. The Virginia constitution was not fundamental, he argued, because it had not emanated from the body politic. He condemned the proceedings of the "delegates and representatives of the good people of Virginia" on the ground that they had not been especially chosen by the people for the particular purpose of drafting a fundamental instrument. Since the constitution was the work of the legislature it stood on the same level as any legislative enactment. Instead of the

[17] *Thomas Jefferson*, p. 204. See *supra*, Ch. V.

legislature deriving power from the fundamental law the constitution had its source in the legislature. Thus the basic principle of constitutional government had been violated.

Consequently, he reasoned "that if . . . the legislature assumes executive and judicial powers, no opposition is likely to be made; nor, if made, can it be effectual; because in that case they may put their proceedings in the form of an act of assembly, which will render them obligatory on the other branches. They have accordingly in many instances decided rights which should have been left to the judiciary controversy; and the direction of the executive, during the whole time of their session, is becoming habitual and familiar."[18]

In the Convention, 1787, George Mason reiterated this position taken by Jefferson. Respecting the mode of ratification, he contended, that it must be determined by the nature of the instrument itself. Since it was fundamental law it was superior to state legislatures as well as to the departments created by it. Thus, it must be ratified by the sovereign body politic. "The legislatures," he argued, "have no power to ratify it. They are the mere creatures of the State Constitutions, and cannot be greater than their creators. . . . Whither must we resort? To the people with whom all power remains that has not been given up in the Constitutions derived from them. Another strong reason was that admitting the Legislatures to have a competent authority, it would be wrong to refer the plan to them, because succeeding Legislatures having equal authority could undo the acts of their predecessors,

[18] Jefferson, *Writings*, III, 225. See also Thach, *op. cit.*, p. 50.

and the National Government would stand in each State on the weak and tottering foundation of an Act of Assembly. This was a remaining consideration of some weight. In some of the States the Governments were (not) derived from the clear and undisputed authority of the people. This was the case in Virginia. Some of the best & wisest citizens considered the Constitution as established by an assumed authority."[19]

Likewise, James Madison on this occasion observed that the legislatures were incompetent to ratify the Constitution; and furthermore "it would be a novel & dangerous doctrine that a Legislature could change the Constitution under which it held its existence. . . . He considered the difference between a system founded on the legislatures only, and one founded on the people, to be the true difference between a *league* or *treaty*, and a *Constitution*. The former in point of *moral obligation* might be as inviolable as the latter. In point of *political operation*, there were two important distinctions in favor of the latter. . . . The doctrine laid down by the law of Nations in the case of treaties is that a breach of any one article by any of the parties, frees the other parties from their engagements. In the case of a union of people under one Constitution, the nature of the pact has always been understood to exclude such an interpretation." He observed further that a legislative enactment might supersede a treaty, but an act contrary to the constitution "established by the people themselves, would be considered by the Judges as null & void."[20] Although Madison lists no authority for this doctrine it is interesting that Charles

[19] *Records of the Federal Convention of 1787*, II, 88.
[20] *Ibid.*, pp. 92-93.

Cotesworth Pinckney, in the South Carolina ratifying convention, discussed the same subject and quoted from Vattel and Burlamaqui. He described the latter as one "of great reputation on political law."[21]

In *The Federalist* Madison described the Constitution as the sole source of governmental power and as depending entirely upon the people. "As the people are the only legitimate fountain of power, and it is from them that the constitutional charter, under which the several branches of government hold their power, is derived, it seems strictly consonant to the republican theory to recur to the same original authority, not only whenever it may be necessary to enlarge, diminish, or new-model the powers of the government, but also whenever any one of the departments may commit encroachments on the chartered authorities of the others."[22]

In the controversy growing out of the Massachusetts Constitution of 1778, the inhabitants of Ipswich drafted the *Essex Result*. It is conceded to have been chiefly the work of Theophilus Parsons. He was not unacquainted with Burlamaqui. Those who studied law under him were required to read *Natural and Politic Law*. One of the points stressed in the *Essex Result* was the fundamental nature and character of a constitution. It derived its authority from the people. The committee inquired as to "what principles and in what manner the supreme power of the state thus composed of the powers of the several individuals thereof may be formed, modelled, and exerted in a republic, so that every member of the state may enjoy political liberty. This is called by some *the ascer-*

[21] Jonathan Elliot, *The Debates in the Several State Conventions* (5 vols. Philadelphia, J. B. Lippincott and Co., 1836), IV, 273.
[22] *The Federalist*, No. 48.

taining of the political law of the state. Let it now be called *the formation of a constitution.*"[23]

James Iredell stated concisely the American concept in the following sentence: "It will not be denied, I suppose, that the Constitution is a *Law of the State,* as well as an act of Assembly, with this difference only, that it is the *fundamental* law and unalterable by the legislature, which derives all its power from it."[24]

Justice Story was able to get a fair perspective of the Constitution. He was able to see the full development and consummation of the concept of fundamental law. Consequently, the relation of Burlamaqui to this concept in its finished form can best be shown by observing the statements of Story and the authorities which he cites. He was familiar with the writings of Burlamaqui, (1), as a student in Harvard, (2), as he had access to it in the Library of the Supreme Court, (3), as law professor at Harvard, and, (4), as he frequently cited him.

Of the theory of consent as a basis of government, Story wrote that "the doctrine maintained by many eminent writers upon public law in modern times is that civil society has its foundation in a voluntary consent or submission; and, therefore, it is often said to depend upon a social compact of the people composing the nation."[25] For this statement he cited Wilson's *Law Lectures,* Volume I, pages 304 to 305; Blackstone's *Commentaries,* Volume I, pages 47 to 48; Vattel, Book One, Chapter One, paragraphs 1 and 2; and Burlamaqui, *Politic Law,* Chapters Two, Three and Four. It should be noted that the passages

[23] Theophilus Parsons, *Memoirs* (T. Parsons, Jr., ed., Boston, Ticknor and Fields, 1859), p. 367.

[24] *Life and Correspondence of James Iredell* (2 vols. Griffith J. McRee, ed., New York, D. Appleton and Company, 1857), II, 148.

[25] *Commentaries on the Constitution of the United States,* I, 225.

to which he referred in Wilson and Blackstone were taken originally from Burlamaqui and that Vattel was a student of Burlamaqui in the University of Geneva. Moreover, in defining the state, Story paraphrased Burlamaqui to the effect that the state is "a multitude of people united together by a common interest, and by common laws, to which they submit with one accord."[26]

In his definition of a constitution he relied solely upon Burlamaqui. "A constitution is in fact," wrote Story, "a fundamental law or basis of government, and falls strictly within the definition of law as given by Mr. Justice Blackstone. It is a rule of action prescribed by the supreme power of the state, regulating the rights and duties of the whole community. It is a *rule*, as contradistinguished from a temporary or sudden order; permanent, uniform and universal. It is also called a rule, to distinguish it from a compact or agreement; for a compact (he adds) is a promise proceeding from us, law is a command directed to us. The language of a compact is, I will or will not do this; that of a law is, thou shalt or shalt not do it."[27] As authorities he cited Blackstone's *Commentaries*, Volume I, pages 38, 44, 45, and Burlamaqui's *Politic Law*, Part I, Chapter VIII, page 48, paragraphs 3, 4 and 5.

2

Another fundamental concept of the Americans in establishing a constitutional government was that of checks and balances. This was to be effected by a separation of powers, both functional and personal, into coördinate de-

[26] *Ibid.*; Story wrote ". . . or as Burlamaqui gives it." See *Politic Law*, Pt. I, Ch. IV, par. ix, p. 25.

[27] Story, *Commentaries*, I, 236.

partments. Thinking solely in terms of a limited government this further restriction upon the rulers was readily seized upon by the Americans. True, the fundamental law was the source of all governmental power, but if this delegated power could be divided by the constitution into well-defined departments it would further restrict the exercise of that power. In order to make this concept of checks and balances effective it was necessary for each of the departments to be coördinate; that is, that they should draw all power from the same source—the constitution. This, as they saw it, was a particular check imposed within the greater restraining law upon the exercise of power by each department.

This peculiarly American application of the concept of checks and balances had been stated explicitly by Burlamaqui in his *Politic Law*. In explaining the concept of coördinate departments, he concluded that "it is by such precautions as these that a nation really limits the authority she confers on the sovereign, and secures her liberty. For . . . civil liberty ought to be accompanied not only with a right of insisting on the sovereign's making a due use of his authority, but moreover with a moral certainty that this right shall have its effect."[28]

Locke's statement of this concept was far from the American practice. He never formulated the underlying theory of the American concept that it was a limiting principle. He used the phrase "checks and balances" only once and then incidentally. His suggested separation was a functional one only. Furthermore, he provided for two departments only—the legislative and executive. The latter was subordinate to the former. Moreover, he justi-

[28] *Politic Law*, Pt. I, Ch. VII, par. xliv, p. 59. See *supra*, Ch. III, for a discussion of his concept.

fied the creation of the executive branch by the legislative upon the grounds of utility.

Without developing the American constitutional principle, Montesquieu, probably the most quoted writer on this concept,[29] merely presented the idea of separation into legislative, executive, and judicial. He set forth this basic idea of eighteenth-century politics, but denied immediately the American idea of coördinate departments. The judiciary, he declared, was subordinate to the legislative and executive. And, he did not state that the last two were co-equal. Moreover, like Locke, he failed to develop the American type of fundamental law. Consequently, he had no foundation upon which to construct a system of coordinate departments. It is not contended that Montesquieu was not accepted authoritatively by the Americans. It is maintained, though, that the Americans were forced to read into Montesquieu their own peculiar application of the idea.[30] Whereas, in the teachings of Burlamaqui they found an express statement of the very position for which they contended. In view of the wide dissemination of his work in America, it may be submitted that he contributed to this concept.

A representative statement of the early American idea of the concept of checks and balances and separation of powers is to be found in the writings of James Otis, 1764. "It is evidently contrary to the first principles of reason," he declared, "that supreme *unlimited* power should be in the hands of one man."[31] Furthermore, he was unwilling

---

[29] *The Federalist*, No. 46. "The Oracle who is always consulted and cited on this subject is the celebrated Montesquieu."

[30] Wright, "The Origin of the Separation of Powers in America," *Economica*, XIII (May, 1933), 169 *et seq.*

[31] Mullett, "Some Political Writings of James Otis," *University of Missouri Studies*, IV (July, 1929), p. 53.

to place unlimited power in the hands of a number of men. The constitution was to serve as a restraint upon all governmental authority.[32] Edward Bernard in 1766 declared that the lodging of legislative and executive functions in the same hand would inevitably "tend to tyranny."[33] It was the opinion of Jonas Clark that the constitution must determine the "departments and powers of government" in order to guarantee to the individual his rights and privileges.[34] Likewise, James Dana observed that the Americans might be "prejudiced by education" in regard to this principle, "but all history assures us, that when the powers of government have been lodged with a single person the care of the public has not been the object of pursuit." However, with a clear division of powers there "is an effectual check to that insupportable pride and boundless ambition, which have slain millions."[35]

In his letter to Richard Henry Lee, 1775, John Adams commented that "a legislative, an executive, and a judicial power comprehend the whole of what is meant and understood by government. It is balancing each of these powers against the other two, that the efforts in human nature towards tyranny can alone be checked and restrained, and any degree of freedom preserved in the constitution."[36] He labored for the establishment of this principle in the state constitutions. It is in his Model Constitution and also stated clearly in the Massachusetts Constitution of 1780.

[32] James K. Hosmer, *The Life of Thomas Hutchinson*, p. 67. He observed that "Otis . . . in exposing and satirizing as absurd and improper the union in one public man of functions judicial, executive, and legislative, was speaking by the book. He was one of the few men in America at that time familiar with Montesquieu's doctrine, afterwards so famous."

[33] *Election Sermon*, p. 13.

[34] *Election Sermon* (1781), p. 9.

[35] James Dana, *Election Sermon* (1779), p. 19.

[36] *Works*, IV, 285.

"In the government of this commonwealth, the legislative department shall never exercise the executive and judicial powers, or either of them. The executive shall never exercise the legislative and judicial powers, or either of them. The judicial shall never exercise the legislative or executive powers, or either of them: to the end it may be a government of laws, and not of men."

Among other passages in his copy of Burlamaqui, Adams noted the following: "As the different branches are not committed to a single person, but lodged in different hands, the power of those who have a share in the government is thereby restrained; and as they are thus a check to each other, this produces such a balance of authority as secures the public weal and the liberty of the individuals."[37] And he may have read that "this partition produces a balance of power, which places the different bodies of the state in such a mutual dependence, as retains every one who has a share in the sovereign authority within the bounds which the law prescribes to them, by which means the public liberty is secured."[38]

The Reverend Samuel Cooper praised the constitution of Massachusetts upon the institution of the new government, 1780, because "it effectually makes the people the keepers of their own liberties, with whom they are certainly safest: How nicely it poises the powers of government, in order to render them so far as human foresight can, what God ever designed they should be, powers only to do good: How happily it guards on the one hand against anarchy and confusion, and on the other against tyranny and oppression: How carefully it separates the legislative from the executive power, a point essential to liberty. How

[37] *Politic Law*, Pt. II, Ch. I, par. xxvi, p. 77.
[38] *Ibid.*, Pt. I, Ch. VII, par. 1, p. 61.

wisely it has provided for the impartial execution of the laws by the independent situation of the judges; a matter of capital moment, and without which the freedom of a constitution in other respects might be often delusory."[39]

Theophilus Parsons condemned the Massachusetts Constitution of 1778 for not guaranteeing the concept of checks and balances through the separation of power into coördinate departments. "The supreme power," he wrote, "is considered as including the legislative, judicial, and executive power. A little attention to the subject will convince us that these three powers ought to be in different hands, and independent of one another, and so balanced, and each having that check upon the other that their independence shall be preserved. If the three powers are united, the government will be absolute, *whether these powers are in the hands of one or a large number.*"[40]

The Virginia Constitution, 1776, paid lip-service to the concept of checks and balances and the principle of separation of powers. "The legislative, executive, and judiciary departments shall be separate and distinct," it read, "so that neither exercises the powers properly belonging to the other; nor shall any person exercise power of more than one of them at the same time."

Jefferson, in voicing his criticism of this constitution, was specific in pointing out that all the power resulted to the legislature. The departments should not only be distinct but coördinate, that is, they should have a means of preserving their independence. This was not a Lockean concept. The government Jefferson was condemning was a prototype of that advocated by Locke. The principle of coördinate departments was interwoven with Jefferson's

[39] *Election Sermon* (1780), p. 28.
[40] *Memoirs*, p. 368.

concept of fundamental law. The reason for the supreme legislature in Virginia was the method of adopting the constitution, he argued. There was no foundation upon which to build a system of coördinate departments. Admitting, nevertheless, that the constitution recognized the three departments he held "that all the powers of government . . . result to the legislative body. The concentrating of these in the same hands is precisely the definition of despotic government. It will be no alleviation that these powers will be exercised by a plurality of hands, and not by a single one. 173 despots would surely be as oppressive as one." He deplored the fact that no legal check was placed upon the legislature. "When, therefore," he wrote, "it is considered that there is no legal obstacle to the assumption by the assembly of all the powers, legislative, executive, and judiciary . . . surely the people will say . . . that they will not acknowledge as laws any acts not considered and assented to by the major part of their delegates." Finally, he concluded, there was no foundation for this condition "but the defect before developed, that there being no barrier between the legislative, executive, and judiciary departments, the legislature may seize the whole: that having seized it, and possessing a right to fix their own quorum, they may reduce that quorum to one, whom they may call a chairman, speaker, dictator, or by any other name they please."[41]

Jefferson's solution of the problem was similar to that of Burlamaqui; that is, that the departments must be coordinate and, thereby, derive their power from the same source—the constitution which is an emanation from the sovereign body politic rather than from the legislature. The proper remedy, he said, "is a convention to fix the

[41] *Writings*, II, 162-65.

constitution, to amend its defects, to bind up the several branches of government by certain laws which, when they transgress, their acts shall become nullities, to render unnecessary an appeal to the people, or, in other words, a rebellion."[42]

James Wilson, too, conceived the principle of checks and balances as a limiting force upon governmental authority. Like Jefferson, he declared the only method of insuring its proper operation was to establish coördinate departments. Independent, coördinate departments were necessary to check the prejudices, passions, and habits of men. Unchecked power in any man's hand was dangerous and led ultimately to tyranny.[43] He did not, however, allow this observation to dull his sight as a practical man trying to establish a workable system. Absolute independence of the departments was not essential to accomplish the limiting principle and, he observed, interdependence would not defeat the end if the jurisdiction were well defined in the fundamental law.[44] He had no sympathy with the arguments of Blackstone and Locke for the supreme legislature. He had witnessed this system in practice and he was a far better student of Burlamaqui than of either of them.[45]

Hamilton, also, advocated the concept of checks and balances based upon coördinate departments. In *The Federalist*, Number 50, he explained cogently this popular American idea. "In order to lay a due foundation," he stated, "for that separate and distinct exercise of the different powers of government which to a certain extent

[42] *Ibid.*, p. 167.
[43] *Works* (Andrews, ed.), I, 352-55.
[44] *Ibid.*, p. 366.
[45] *Ibid.*, p. 170.

is admitted on all hands to be essential to the preservation of liberty, it is evident that each department should have a will of its own, and consequently should be so constituted that the members of each should have as little agency as possible in the appointment of the members of the others." Advancing a means of securing an effective check, he concluded: "But the great security against a gradual concentration of the several powers in the same department consists in giving to those who administer each department the necessary constitutional means and personal motives to resist encroachments of the others."

In the New York ratifying convention, 1788, Hamilton demonstrated the relation of the end of the state and the concept of checks and balances. "Has philosophy suggested," he asked, "has experience taught, that such a government ought not to be trusted with everything necessary for the good of society? When you have divided and nicely balanced the departments of government, when you have strongly connected the virtue of your rulers with their interest, when, in short, you have rendered your system as perfect as human forms can be, you must place confidence, you must give power."[46] Finally, he was persuaded that "the true principle of government is this—make the system complete in its structure, give a perfect proportion and balance to its parts, and the powers you give it will never affect your security."[47]

Another who was convinced of the importance of this concept to the American constitutional system was James Madison. In the Convention and elsewhere he advanced the idea. "If it be essential," he argued on the floor of the Convention, "to the preservation of liberty that the legisl:

[46] *Works*, II, 61.
[47] *Ibid.*, p. 53.

execut: & judiciary powers be separate, it is essential
to a maintenance of the separation that they should be independent of each other. The Executive could not be independent of the Legislature if dependent on the pleasure of that branch for re-appointment. Why was it
determined that the Judges should not hold their places
by such a tenure: Because they might be tempted to cul-
tivate the Legislature, by an undue complaisance, and
thus render the Legislature the virtual expositor, as well
as the maker of the laws. In like manner a dependence of
the Executive on the Legislature would render it the Executor as well as the maker of laws."[48]

But it is in *The Federalist*, Numbers 46, 47 and 48, that
he expounds the theory and application of the principle.
After reviewing its application and result in the state constitutions he observed pragmatically that "after discrim-
inating, therefore, in theory, the several classes of power
as they may in their nature be legislative, executive, or
judiciary, the next and most difficult task is to provide
some practical security for each against the invasion of
the others. What this security ought to be is the great
problem to be solved.

"Will it be sufficient to mark, with precision, the
boundaries of these departments, in the constitution of the
government and to trust to these parchment barriers
against the encroaching spirit of power? This is the security which appears to have been principally relied on by
the compilers of most of the American constitutions; but
experience assures us that the efficacy of the provision
has been greatly overrated, and some more adequate defence is indispensably necessary for the more feeble

[48] *Records of the Federal Convention of 1787*, II, 34.

against the more powerful members of the government."[49]

More security than that afforded by a fundamental law was thus demanded by Madison. Burlamaqui was confronted with the same problem as were all the constitutionalists of the eighteenth century. Burlamaqui's solution was to permit each department to act independently of the others but always within the fundamental law. A "precaution" in addition to the constitution, he wrote, was to regulate "the government by a fundamental law in such a manner as to commit the exercise of the different parts of the supreme power to different persons or bodies who may act independently of each other in regard to the rights committed to them but still subordinate to the laws from which those rights are derived."[50] Moreover, he advocated the establishment of an institution for the specific purpose of guarding the constitution, thereby restraining the aggressive activities of any department.

Madison relied upon Montesquieu for this concept if we are to judge from the numerous citations to him. However, Montesquieu never outlined a scheme with all the implications of that of Madison. The most effective and persistent source upon him was the experience in the states. Yet, Burlamaqui, it may be maintained, contributed to the general acceptance. Madison was not unfamiliar with the Swiss jurist. And in his *Helvidius* papers, Madison cited him as an authority in defence of the powers of the executive.[51] The striking similarity of the reasoning of Madison to that of Burlamaqui is demonstrated in the following extract from *The Federalist:* "As the people are

[49] *The Federalist*, No. 47.
[50] *Politic Law*, Pt. II, Ch. I, par. xix, p. 75.
[51] *Works*, I, 611.

the only legitimate fountain of power, and it is from them that the constitutional charter, under which the several branches of government hold their power, is derived, it seems strictly consonant to the republican theory to recur to the same original authority, not only whenever it may be necessary to enlarge, diminish, or new-model the powers of the government, but also whenever any one of the departments may commit encroachments on the chartered authorities of the others."[52]

This procedure, in the opinion of Madison, was too laborious and possessed certain defects. As a practical and more workable process of government, he, like Burlamaqui, proposed the establishment of an institutional check upon the exercise of governmental power. This would not only protect the fundamental law but would guarantee, so far as any mechanical means could, the maintenance of the proper balance among the departments. The result would be the greatest protection to the liberties of the people.

3

The Americans consummated their interpretation of the doctrine of limited government by erecting an institutional check to the legislature. Basically, the demand for controls upon this branch of the government arose from a fear of too much democracy. In the governmental structure the legislature presented the most vulnerable point for democratic attack. This had been demonstrated clearly by the experiences with the colonial and state governments. Much of the criticism of the governmental structure of the states before 1787 and its operation was directed at the powerful legislatures. The theoretical concepts of funda-

[52] No. 48.

mental law and checks and balances had not proved in practice sufficiently effectual limits to the forces of democracy. Consequently, during the early period of American constitutional development, there was a search for a more effective means of curbing the excesses of democracy. Theoretically it was stated as a demand for the protection of the constitution in its original form and intent, except as it might be changed through the legal procedure of amendment. The idea of a written constitution presupposes the concept of stability and the will to mold indefinitely the structure and the character of a political system within well-defined principles. The Framers took all the precautions possible to prevent a successful attack upon the fundamental law.

Political organization can have substance and vitality only when it is consonant with economic life. Constitutional government was the political system which fitted most closely the demands of an industrial civilization and a nascent capitalism. Judicial review has proved to be the crowning achievement of the American conservative mind. The initiators of the idea of an institutional check upon the legislature could not have conceived of its ultimate value to capitalism. It is highly improbable that the most reactionary of its early proponents could have foreseen by the greatest stretch of the imagination the obstinacy of the Supreme Court to social reform.

In the development of the principle of judicial review the Americans began with a fundamental law emanating from the sovereign-body politic. This was the sole source of governmental power; consequently, it was a limitation. To be an effective control, they argued, some body or department should have the power of guardianship over the constitution. Burlamaqui stated this idea as follows: that the state should take precautions actually to "limit the authority she confers on the sovereign," not only with insistence upon the sovereign's using the power in the manner prescribed but "with moral certainty that this right shall have its effect." The provisions made by the people must not be "easily eluded."[53]

With Burlamaqui this was not to be a stronghold of reactionary thought. It was not an institution which stood guard over the rights of vested interests only. The all-inclusive rule of social good and social necessity as determined by individual happiness would preclude any act of this body which would nullify social progress. Burlamaqui, however, accepted one of the fallacies of the Whig school of thought. He ignored the personal equation in politics.

The early growth of institutional control of the legislature followed two plans. The one more widely used was to rely upon the political and moral responsibility of the legislators and the judges, especially the latter. It may be noted historically that the judges in several of the states assumed early the responsibility of protecting the constitutions.[54] In three of the states, Pennsylvania, New York, and New Hampshire, an especial body was set up for the express purpose of guarding the constitution against legislative and executive encroachment. This was assumed, apparently, to be a function of such a peculiar nature that it could not be left to one of the regular departments of government. It might be argued that this is far more consistent with American constitutional theory, especially the

[53] *Politic Law*, Pt. I, Ch. VII, par. xliv, p. 50. It should be noted that John Adams marked this passage, James Wilson quoted it, and others referred to it.

[54] Haines, *The American Doctrine of Judicial Supremacy*, p. 12.

idea of coördinate departments, than is the now accepted principle that it is a function of the judicial branch.

The Pennsylvania constitution of 1776 provided for a Council of Censors which should meet every seven years. It was composed of two persons from each city and county of the state. The people were considered the final interpreters of the fundamental law. The function assigned to this institutional check was "to inquire whether the constitution has been preserved inviolate in every part; and whether the legislative and executive branches of government have performed their duty as guardians of the people, or assumed to themselves, or exercised other or greater powers than they are entitled to by the constitution."[55] Likewise, the Vermont constitution, 1777, provided for a similar institution. However, its work was confined solely to advising because the constitution of that state was not promulgated as a fundamental law until 1796.

Of the three states establishing the constitutional body, the New York Council of Revision, 1777, was the most effective. This Council, composed of the governor, the chancellor, and the judges of the supreme court, was given the task of exercising a qualified veto over laws which might be deemed by it "inconsistent with the spirit of the constitution or with the public good." This Council, which was expected to serve as a check upon the legislative in the capacity of a vetoing agency, came to be the guardian of the constitution as a fundamental law. As early as 1778 the Council declared against a bill because it was "inconsistent with the spirit of the constitution of this state." As late as 1820, "the legislature recommended a convention,"

---

[55] F. N. Thorpe, *The Federal and State Constitutions, Colonial Charters, and Other Organic Laws of the States,* V, 3091, sec. 46.

said Haines, "without submitting the question to the voters. When the bill was referred to the Council, the measure was returned with the observation that 'the difficulty of acceding to such a measure of reform, without the previous approbation of the constituents of the government, presses with peculiar force and with painful anxiety upon the Council of Revision, which was instituted for the express purpose of guarding the Constitution against the passage of laws inconsistent with its spirit.' "[56]

Thomas Jefferson, in his *Notes on Virginia*, was favorable to this type of institution to protect the fundamental law from the encroachments of the legislature. He proposed that the members be chosen by the legislature for seven years and be ineligible for reëlection. Its function was to advise whether or not the fundamental law had been strictly adhered to by the rulers and particularly by the legislature.[57]

Although the idea of a fundamental law was the common point of departure, and so stated by many of the leaders of the later constitutional period (and more often assumed), the practical effect was to establish a secure check upon the legislature. The striking characteristic of the period was to limit the exercise of legislative power. All possible limits upon this—in practice—all-powerful department of government were becoming axiomatic. The Americans had entered the debate with Great Britain with the fundamental notion that all legislative power was curbed, first, by the law of nature and, secondly, by the constitution. In addition they had demanded the concept of checks and balances which could be effected through the separation of powers into coördinate departments.

[56] Haines, *The American Doctrine of Judicial Supremacy*, pp. 134-35, 136.
[57] Jefferson, *Works*, II, 290.

However, by 1787 these had not proven a sufficiently effective guarantee, except in those states in which judges had assumed the power of judicial review or in New York with its Council of Revision.

Alexander Hamilton gave a clear and succinct statement of the doctrine of judicial review as it had developed by 1788. In *The Federalist* papers he accepted it as a proper function of the courts. "The interpretation of the laws is the proper and peculiar province of the courts. A constitution is, in fact, and must be regarded by the judges as a fundamental law. It therefore belongs to them to ascertain its meaning, as well as the meaning of any particular act proceeding from the legislative body. If there should happen to be an irreconcilable variance between the two, that which has the superior obligation and validity ought, of course, to be preferred; or, in other words, the constitution ought to be preferred to the statute, the intention of the people to the intention of their agents. . . . They [the judges] ought to regulate their decisions by the fundamental laws, rather than by those which are not fundamental."[58]

The embryo of this principle may be evidenced as early as the 1760's in America. The Reverend Benjamin Stevens, paraphrasing Burlamaqui, insisted that the constitution partitioned sovereignty into different branches and specifically curbed the legislative and the executive departments so that they "will enact" and "enforce" such laws "and such only" as are agreeable to the grant of power and to their safety and happiness.[59]

James Otis in 1761 stated positively that the legislature was subservient to the fundamental law and the law of

---

[58] *The Federalist*, No. 78.
[59] *Election Sermon* (1765), p. 51.

nature. "Thus reason and the constitution," he declared, "are both against this writ. Let us see what authority there is for it. . . . No acts of Parliament can establish such a writ; though it should be made in the very words of the petition it would be void. An act against the constitution is void."[60] Again, he wrote that "these are their bounds, which by God and nature are fixed, hitherto have they a right to come, and no further. . . . These are the first principles of law and justice, and the great barriers of a free state, and of the British Constitution in particular. To say the Parliament is absolute and arbitrary is a contradiction."[61]

Justice Wythe, who had been teaching Burlamaqui's works in William and Mary since 1779, declared in the case of *Commonwealth* v. *Caton:* "Nay more, if the whole legislature, an event to be deprecated, should attempt to overleap the bounds prescribed to them by the people, I, in administering the public justice of the country will meet the united powers, at my seat in this tribunal, and, pointing, to the constitution, will say to them, here is the limit of your authority; and hither shall you go, but no further."[62]

James Iredell came directly to the point that this was a concept of a practical check upon the legislature in addition to others already imposed. "It was, of course," he wrote, "to be considered how to impose restrictions on the legislature that might still leave it free to all useful purposes but at the same time guard against the abuse of unlimited power, which was not to be trusted, without the

[60] Cited in Adams, *Works*, II, 525.
[61] C. F. Mullett, "Some Political Writings of James Otis," *University of Missouri Studies*, IV (July, 1929), 70.
[62] *Commonwealth* v. *Caton*, 4 Call. 8 (1782).

most imminent danger, to any man or body of men on earth. . . . I have therefore no doubt but that the power of the Assembly is limited and defined by the Constitution. It is a creature of the Constitution."[63]

Hamilton developed logically the principle of an especially restricted legislative power in *The Federalist*. "By a limited Constitution I understand one which contains certain specified exceptions to the legislative authority, such, for instance, as that it shall pass no bills of attainder, no *ex post facto* laws, and the like. Limitations of this kind can be preserved in practice in no other way than through the medium of courts of justice, whose duty it must be to declare all acts contrary to the manifest tenor of the Constitution void. Without this, all the reservations of particular rights or privileges would amount to nothing."[64]

Similarly, James Wilson pointed out that natural and revealed law were restrictions upon the legislative body. However, following the line of reasoning of Burlamaqui, there was a fundamental law or constitution which further restricted the legislative authority. "To control the power and conduct of the legislature," Wilson wrote, "by an overruling constitution was an improvement in the science and practice of government reserved to the American states. . . . The truth is that in our governments the supreme, absolute and uncontrollable power remains in the people. As our constitutions are superior to our legislatures, so the people are superior to our constitutions."[65] Moreover, Wilson was clearly following the Swiss jurist when he held that "the effects of its [legislature] extravagances may be prevented, sometimes by the executive,

[63] *Life and Correspondence of James Iredell*, II, 145-46.
[64] No. 78.
[65] Wilson, *Works* (Andrews, ed.), I, 415. In his *Commentaries*, 1787.

sometimes by the judicial authority of the government, sometimes even by a private citizen, and at all times, by the superintending power of the people at large."[66] Like Burlamaqui, he argued that the individual citizen was not bound to obey an unconstitutional law. However, if the citizen's judgment was wrong he must abide by the consequence.

In the constitutional convention Wilson, ably supported by Madison, strongly urged the adoption of a Council of Revision. The basis of argument was suggestive of Burlamaqui. After the discussion had been closed, Wilson argued for a reconsideration on the grounds that "the judiciary ought to have an opportunity of remonstrating against projected encroachments on the people as well as on themselves. It has been said that the judges, as expositors of the laws, would have an opportunity of defending their constitutional rights. There was weight in this observation, but this power of the judges did not go far enough. Laws may be unjust, may be unwise, may be dangerous, may be destructive, and yet not be so unconstitutional as to justify the judges in refusing to give them effect. Let them have a share in the revisionary power, and they will have an opportunity of taking notice of these characters of a law and of counteracting, by the weight of their opinions, the improper views of the legislature."[67]

It would seem that Wilson, Madison and others in the convention were not wholly satisfied with allowing the court alone to exercise this function. However, Wilson pointed out that the exercise of this function by the courts did not violate the concept of a division of governmental powers into coördinate departments. Here he enunciated

[66] *Ibid.*, pp. 189 ff.
[67] *Records of the Constitutional Convention of 1787*, II, 73.

the basis of the argument of John Marshall in the famous case of *Marbury* v. *Madison*. "When repugnant commands are delivered by two different authorities," he wrote, "one inferior and the other superior, which must be obeyed? When the courts of justice obey the superior authority, it can not be said with propriety that they control the inferior one; they only declare, as it is their duty to declare, that this inferior one is controlled by the other, which is superior. They do not repeal the act of parliament; they pronounce it void, because contrary to an overruling law. From that overruling law they receive the authority to pronounce such a sentence." Pursuing the argument further, Wilson contended that it was the duty of the court to determine what is the law of the land. "This is the necessary result," he argued, "of the distribution of power made, by the constitution, between the legislative and the judicial departments. The same constitution is the supreme law for both." And he concluded in a sentence which epitomized this phase of the American concept of an institutional check: "What a noble guard against legislative despotism!"[68]

It was left for John Marshall to give classic form to this polemic. "The powers of the legislature are defined and limited; and that those limits may not be mistaken or forgotten, the Constitution is written. To what purpose are powers limited, and to what purpose is that limitation committed to writing, if these limits may, at any time, be passed by those intended to be restrained? The distinction between a government with limited and unlimited powers is abolished, if those limits do not confine the persons on whom they are imposed, and if acts prohibited and acts

[68] Wilson, *Works* (Andrews, ed.), I, 415-17. Cf. Hamilton in *The Federalist*, No. 78.

allowed are of equal obligation." Moreover, if unconstitutional legislative acts are obliging, this "would be giving
to the legislature a practical and real omnipotence with
the same breath which professes to restrict their powers
within narrow limits. It is prescribing limits and declaring
that those limits may not be passed at pleasure. That it thus
reduces to nothing what we have deemed the greatest improvement on political institutions, a written constitution,
would of itself be sufficient in America, where written
constitutions have been viewed with so much reverence,
for rejecting the construction. But the peculiar expressions
of the Constitution of the United States furnish additional
arguments in favor of its rejection."[69]

[69] *Marbury* v. *Madison*, 1 Cranch 176 (1803).

CONCLUSION

THIS STUDY has demonstrated certain notable contributions of Jean Jacques Burlamaqui to the field of political philosophy and particularly to the science of constitutional government.

He was the first modern political philosopher to depart from the orthodox teachings of the mediaevalists and the contractualists in respect to the nature of the state. The broad philosophical principles upon which he founded the state were not conceived within the narrow limits which had restricted the philosophical thought of his predecessors. They were conceived in the manner of the ancient Greeks. The state to him was an institution which made possible the development of man's faculties to the utmost, which aided him in the attainment of the better self, which permitted the realization of the end for which man was created, namely, happiness. Burlamaqui was the first modern philosopher to enumerate happiness as a natural right—a right which forms the basis of the state. In his hands, the state became a positive institution—an institution created and maintained only so long as it better enabled man to attain the ultimate realization of his end, happiness—and was not merely a negative institution which served only in the capacity of a policeman. The state was an institution natural to man and not a self-imposed organization whose sole basis of existence was convention.

This was a concept of the state foreign to the political theorizing from Aristotle to Burlamaqui. Thus, to Burlamaqui should go the applause which has been given unstintingly to Montesquieu and Rousseau for setting modern political philosophy aright and founding it upon the true principles which had been enunciated by Aristotle. This one concept—the positive nature of the state and government—is sufficient, if he had developed no others, to rank him with the great political philosophers of the seventeenth and eighteenth centuries.

Burlamaqui was, moreover, one of the forerunners of the modern objectivist school, inasmuch as he held that law was not obliging solely because it had issued from the organ which the people had by consent established. In order for it to oblige the individual it must not only proceed from the proper authority but in its content it must be also of some utility. Law could not be promulgated only to restrain the individual. To be obliging, law must lay an internal and external obligation. It was a positive rule of the state which further aided man in the realization of the better life.

In the field of constitutional theory Burlamaqui contributed fundamental ideas of immeasurable consequence to the subsequent development of constitutional government. Particularly is there a striking similarity between his theoretical statement of constitutional principles and the American development. Many of these concepts are not original with Burlamaqui, but the peculiar manner in which he developed them was strikingly new in the science of government.

Burlamaqui formulated the principles of popular sovereignty, of delegated power, of a constitution as a fundamental law, of a personal and functional separation of powers into three independent departments, of a system of checks and balances based upon coördinate departments and, finally, he provided for an institutional guardian of the fundamental law.

He gave the first theoretic statement to the concept of a fundamental law emanating from the sovereign-body politic as the source of all governmental power. He gave expression to the concept that since sovereignty resides in the people they have the power to limit the rulers by a delegation of authority through a constitution. This was a startlingly new development in the idea of fundamental law as it imposed a limitation upon the government in addition to the always present law of nature.

The constitution furnished the basis for a further development of the system of checks and balances operating by means of three coördinate departments of government. To be sure, this idea was old in the time of Burlamaqui. However, the theory underlying the concept of checks and balances had never been so clearly stated. The concept had never possessed in the hands of other philosophers so firm a foundation upon which to rest. Burlamaqui, starting with the fundamental law, conceived of additional limitations to safeguard the exercise of delegated authority. This was accomplished, he held, by a division into legislative, executive, and judicial branches, each looking to the constitution for its particular grant of power. This separation was to be personal and functional. His special contribution to this concept was the principle of coördinate departments, each with the power to protect its independence from the encroachment of the others. On this basis he defended the concept as an effectual check upon the exercise of authority.

Finally, he adumbrated the American concept of judicial review. The fundamental law created three coördinate departments. Thus, the legislature was limited by the same body as the executive and judicial branches. In order to guarantee the subordination of these departments to the fundamental law, he suggested the establishment of an institution whose sole duty would be to determine when this law had been violated.

In short, Burlamaqui gave the first complete theoretical statement of the entire body of American constitutionalism. There is a striking similarity between the above enumerated constitutional principles and the American. Moreover, his works were authoritative references in the development of constitutional principles in the period after 1760. His wide popularity throughout the formative period of American constitutionalism and the high esteem in which he was held by the formulators of the American concepts bear undisputable testimony to this. This popularity is evidenced in that some sixteen public or society libraries in America secured copies of the work during the years 1757-1800; that the oldest colleges of America possessed copies as early as 1764 and the number on their shelves continued to grow until the close of the first quarter of the nineteenth century. In fact, some twenty-three colleges founded well before or immediately following 1800 procured copies for the students. Moreover, the booksellers and importers of Boston, New York, and Philadelphia had his work in stock. What is more highly indicative of his popularity are the numerous privately owned copies. It has been established that some eighty persons, including practically all the recognized leaders, had copies of the work at some time during the period. The popularity of and esteem for his works are demonstrated by their use in some twelve colleges and universities as a text during the latter half of the eighteenth and the first quarter of the nineteenth centuries. Finally, the comparatively early reprints in America, ultimately reaching the total of seven, definitely establish the demand for his work.

It is particularly significant, however, that in addition to this indirect evidence that he was a highly acceptable source to the Americans, there is ample direct evidence to demonstrate that he was an accepted authority in the field of natural and politic law. The fact that he was cited by name by numerous Americans—ministers, lawyers, statesmen, professors, and laymen—is indisputable evidence that he was a welcome source of thought.

While Burlamaqui was contributory to some of the American concepts, he was in others almost the sole source. The doctrine enunciated in the Declaration of Independence of man's inherent right to the "pursuit of happiness" is traceable to Burlamaqui. The prevailing concept of the state in 1776 that its existence was justified only so long as it aided the individual in the attainment of happiness was thoroughly Burlamaquian. The authorities upon which the Americans might rely for this particular idea were limited to the ancient Greeks and Burlamaqui.

Also, his work was a contributing factor to the general growth of the concept of the state as limited by natural law. He assisted in the development of the consent theory of the state and government. He was especially acceptable to the Americans with his new idea that consent could be employed as a basis for a limited government separate from the state.

On this basis Burlamaqui gave the first theoretical statement of the American doctrine of a fundamental law as something separate and distinct from a higher law. The

Americans did not fail to make use of this doctrine and, in many instances, cited him directly as the source. In a few cases they cited Blackstone who had merely taken the words of Burlamaqui.

He was the first to state the American principle of checks and balances as based upon coördinate departments deriving their power from a constitution. It is true, of course, that Montesquieu was cited frequently for this principle, as well as upon most any concept, yet the American application of it was more strikingly like Burlamaqui.

Lastly, Burlamaqui laid the foundation for the American doctrine of judicial review and suggested the establishment of an organ for the purpose of guarding the fundamental law. With regard to this concept, Burlamaqui constitutes another probable source of the American idea.

This study has demonstrated the striking similarity between Burlamaqui's *Natural and Politic Law* and American constitutional government. It has shown the indirect and direct influence of that work upon American constitutionalism. It places Burlamaqui on equal terms with the conventionally recognized sources of American thought such as Locke, Montesquieu, Blackstone, Coke, and others. Upon the evidence at hand, it may be concluded that Burlamaqui was as popular in America as any of the conventionally cited authorities, he was referred to almost as frequently as were they, and he set forth a better developed constitutional theory than any of them.

APPENDICES

BIOGRAPHICAL NOTE

JEAN JACQUES BURLAMAQUI was born in Geneva, July 19, 1694. His ancestors came originally from an old Italian family of Lucca. At that time the name was spelled Burlamacchi. Due to the long residence of the family in France the spelling was changed. Religious difficulties in Lucca forced the family to emigrate to France in the early years of the sixteenth century. Similar difficulties dogged the steps of the family in its adopted lands. It is known that the Burlamaqui family was attacked in the St. Bartholomew Massacres in 1572. Fortunately they escaped to Austria where they spent some few years before moving to Switzerland.

The Burlamacchi family of Lucca was of noble blood. After emigration members of the family married into the noble families of France and Austria. Little is known of Jean's father except that he was connected with the church at Grenoble and served as Counsellor of State and Secretary of State for several years before his death in 1728.

Jean Jacques was a graduate of the University of Geneva. On completing his course he travelled in England, Holland, and France. He was received at Oxford, and, it is said, "because of his talents," the authorities gave him a *History of the University of Oxford* in two volumes. In Holland he was a guest of Barbeyrac, the translator of the works of Pufendorf and a commentator on Grotius. Upon returning to Geneva he was made professor of natural and civil law in the University at the age of twenty-five. This position he held for some twenty years when ill health forced his resignation. His long service in the University was rewarded by the state with an appointment to the Council of State. This position he held until his untimely death in April, 1748.[1]

Burlamaqui wrote a two-volume work called *Principes du droit naturel et politique*. It was first published in 1747. The work was written and published, he said, because copies of his notes had become scattered and he feared their publication in altered form after his death. The work met with immediate success both at home and abroad. It was translated into numerous languages and went through many editions.

Not a little of this popularity can be attributed to his free, simple, and lucid style. In this respect he stands in bold relief among the philosophers of the seventeenth and eighteenth centuries. Not until the appearance of Rousseau's *Contrat Social* did he have a rival. While Professor Dunning can say justly of the style and method of Grotius that "he illustrates in these respects the best and worst features of the reaction against scholasticism," that "his enunciation of principles is clear, straightforward and concise, and appeals to the intelligence of the untrained as well as of the trained ruler"; [2] it can be said of Burlamaqui that he illustrates all this and more. He goes much farther and breaks with the pedantic style of Grotius, Pufendorf, Hobbes, Sydney and others who perpetuated the style of Grotius. Where Grotius and his followers inserted masses of Latin and Scriptural quotations and footnotes to bolster their argment Burlamaqui sets down his thoughts in simple, readable, and understandable language. The severest critic cannot ascribe pedantic ostentation to him.

This particular characteristic did not go unrewarded. Professor F. de Félice, who edited the works of Burlamaqui in 1766, was much impressed with the style; so much so that he gave it as one justification for selecting the work for publication.[3] This opinion was voiced also by John Clarke, a Boston minister, who said that

[1] "Eloge Historique de M. Burlamaqui," a letter written by Mr. Baulacre, of the library of Geneva, to M. Formey in 1750. (This is contained in the Swiss and French editions of Burlamaqui's works. See *Principes du droit de la nature et des gens*, 8 vols., ed. by Félice, Yverdon, 1766–1768, I, vi.) There is no biography of Burlamaqui.

[2] W. A. Dunning, *Political Theories from Luther to Montesquieu*, p. 162.

[3] J. J. Burlamaqui, *Principes du droit de la nature et des gens* (8 vols., Yverdon, 1766), "Introduction," p. xx, letter to Monsieur Formey.

"his style is much admired for its clearness and purity." [4] In the early nineteenth century Cotelle aptly remarks that "Burlamaqui est le premier auteur qui se soit affranchi du style pédantesque, hérissé de latin et de citations, qui était en usage dans l'ancienne école; le sien est d'une clarté et d'une précision admirable; il ne manque même pas d'élégance et de goût." [5] This was accomplished without any loss to the content or the authority of the work. In the words of Professor de Félice, "Ce libre est clair sans être prolixe, précis sans être défectueux, simple dans toute la force du raisonnement." [6]

[4] John Clarke, *Letters to a Student in the University of Cambridge, Massachusetts.*

[5] J. J. Burlamaqui, *Principes du droit de la nature et des gens, et du droit public général* (2 vols. Cotelle, ed., Paris, Janet et Cotelle, 1821), "Avertissement de l'éditeur," I, iv.

[6] Félice's "Introduction" to his edition of 1766, p. xx.

BIBLIOGRAPHICAL HISTORY

BURLAMAQUI'S ORIGINAL WORKS ARE:

Dissertatio Juridica de Matrimonio. *Genève, Fabre et Barrillot,*
1731.

Principes du droit naturel. *Genève, Barrillot, 1747.*

Principes du droit naturel. *Genève, Barrillot, 1747.*

The first publication of *Principes du droit naturel* contains two
parts: (1) Des principes généraux du droit and (2) Des loix natu-
relles. The second publication under the same title contains three
divisions. The part added in the latter publication is called *Suite*
des principes du droit naturel. The second publication became immediately a two-volume work bearing the title *Principes du droit*
naturel et droit politique. The second volume of this work is divided into four parts, the first three containing in the main his
constitutional theory, and Part IV dealing with the law of nations.

In addition to the original volumes there is an edition of his
notes and lectures collected by his former students and edited by
Félice. This edition has the title *Élémens du droit naturel* (Lausanne, François Grasset, 1775), 360 pp.

SWISS EDITIONS:

(after the originals):

Les principes du droit naturel. *2 vols. Genève, Barrillot et fils,*
1748.

Abrégé du droit naturel. *2 vols. in 1. Genève, Barrillot et fils,*
1750.

Les principes du droit politique. *1 vol. Genève, Barrillot et fils, 1751.*

Same. *1 vol. Genève, Phillibert, 1754.*

Juris Naturalis Elementa. *1 vol. Genève, Phillibert, 1754. Translated into Latin by De Tournes.*

Principes du droit naturel. *2 vols. in 1. Nouve. éd. Genève et Copenhague, Phillibert, 1756.*

Same. *2 vols. in 1. Nouve. éd. Genève et Copenhague, Phillibert, 1762.*

Principes du droit politique. *1 vol. Genève, Phillibert, 1763.*

Principes du droit naturel et politique. *3 vols. Genève, Phillibert, 1764. The component parts of the work are published separately.*

Élémens du droit naturel. *Lausanne, Grasset et Comp., 1783. Ouvrage posthume, publié complet pour la première fois.*

Principes ou élémens du droit politique. *Lausanne, Grasset et Comp., 1784.*

Professor F. de Félice of the faculty of law of Paris edited the works of Burlamaqui together with many notes under the title of *Principes du droit de la nature et des gens avec la suite du droit de la nature*, 8 vols. Yverdon, 1766. Félice included in addition to his notes an introduction, "Historique et critique au droit naturel."

FRENCH EDITIONS:

Principes du droit naturel. *Palais de L'Union, 1771.*

Same. *1 vol. Nouve. éd., revue, corrigée et augmentée de la Déclaration des droits de l'homme. Paris, Guillaume, 1791.*

Élémens du droit naturel, et devoirs de l'homme et du citoyen, tels qu'ils lui sont prescrits par la loi naturelle, traduits du latin de Pufendorf par Barbeyrac, avec les notes du traducteur et le judgement de Leibnitz. *2 vols. in 1. Nouve. éd., edited by Saint-Ange Cotelle. Paris, Janet et Cotelle, 1820. The first 248 pages are Burlamaqui.*

Principes du droit de la nature et des gens. *5 vols. M. Dupin Ed. Paris, Waree, 1820–21.*

Principes du droit de la nature et des gens, et du droit public général. *2 vols. M. Cotelle Ed. Paris, Janet et Cotelle, 1821.*

Élémens du droit naturel. *1 vol. Nouve. éd. Paris, Delestre-Rou-*
lage, 1821.

Same. *1 vol. Nouve. éd. Paris, Brajeus, 1850.*

DUTCH EDITIONS:

Beginsels van het Natuurlyk Regt: waerin de algemeene gronden
van 's menschen pligt, de aert en 't oogmerk der wet, de
zedelykheit onzer daeden, de aenwezendheit van God, de na-
tuur van 't geweten, de gevolgen van deugd en ondeugd, en
de onsterffelykheit der ziele, uit het licht der reden betooged;
midsgaders de gevoelens van Grotius, Pufendorf, Barbeyrac,
Dr. Clarcke, enz. ander overwogen worden. Uit het Fransch
Vertaeld, door Marten Schagen. *1 vol. Haerlem, Jan Bosch,*
1750.

Principes du droit politique. *1 vol. Amsterdam, J. Wetstein, 1751.*

Same. *1 vol. Amsterdam, Chastalian, 1751.*

Beginsels van het Burgerlyk Regt: waerin d'Oirsprong enz. Ook
het Oorlogs-en Vrede-Regt, met de Openbaere Verbonden
en Traktaeten, midsgaders de Voorregten der Ambassadeurs
en Gezanten. Ten vervalge van de Beginselen des Natuur-
lyken Regts. Uit het Fransh Vertaeld. *2 vols. in 1. Haerlem,*
Jan Bosch, 1752.

GERMAN EDITION:

Abhandlung—von dem Willen und der Freyheit des Menschen.
Voir Reinhard. Vergleichung des Lehrgebaudes des Herrn
Pope von der Vollkommenheit der Welt, mit dem System des
Herrn Von Leibnitz. *Leipzig, 1757.*

SWEDISH TRANSLATION:

Stats-Road og Tilforn offentlig Laerere i den Naturlige og Borger-
lige Ret universitetet i Genf. Grundsetninger til Soturens
Ret. *Leipzig, Af det Fransfe obersat ded A. S. Dellgast,*
1757. 1 vol.

ENGLISH EDITIONS:

The Principles of Natural Law. In which the true systems of mo-
rality and civil government are established; and the different
sentiments of Grotius, Hobbes, Pufendorf, Barbeyrac, Locke,
Clarke and Hutchinson occasionally considered. *1 vol. Trans.*
by T. Nugent. London, J. Nourse, 1748.

Same. *1 vol. London, J. Nourse, 1752.*

Principles of Politic Law: Being a sequel to the Principles of Natural Law. *1 vol. London, J. Nourse, 1752.*

Principles of Natural and Politic Law. *2 vols. London, J. Nourse, 1752.*

Second edition. *2 vols. London, J. Nourse, 1763.*

Third edition. *2 vols. London, C. Nourse, 1784.*

Fourth edition. *2 vols. London, C. Nourse, 1789.*

Fifth edition. *2 vols. in 1. London, C. Nourse, 1791.*

Sixth edition. *2 vols. in 1. Oxford, 1807.*

Seventh edition. *2 vols. in 1. Oxford, 1817.*

EDITIONS IN IRELAND:

Principles of Natural and Politic Law. *2 vols. Dublin, 1776.*

Same. Fifth English ed. *2 vols. in 1. Dublin, Rice, 1791.*

Principles of Natural Law. *Dublin, T. V. Morris, 1838. To this is appended "With Questions for Examination. By a graduate of the University."*

Burlamaqui's Natural Law Catechetically Arranged. *Dublin, L. Baden, 1838.*

ITALIAN AND LATIN TRANSLATIONS:

Juris Naturalis Elementa. *1 tome. Venetuis, J. J. B. apud Josephem Bortoli, 1757.*

Principii del Dritto Naturale di J. J. Burlamacchi. *2 tomi. Le Comte Bapt-Creopi l'a traduit en Italien. Venise, 1780.*

Principii del Dritto della Natura e delle Genti. Colla continuazione del dritto della natura aggiunta nell' ultima edizione de' Yverdon. *8 tomi. Tutto notabilmente accresciuto da F. de Félice. Traduzione dal francese. Siena, 1780–1782.*

Juris Naturalis Elementa. *1 tome. Venetuis, Sumptibus Jo: Antonii Pezzano, 1789.*

Principii del Dritto Naturale e Politico. *2 tomi. Traduzione dal francese del C. B. C. Venezia, Battista Pasquali, 1797.*

Principii del Dritto Naturale e Politico. *2 tomi. Traduzione dal francese del C. B. C. Napoli, Da Torchi de Raffaello di Napoli, 1825.*

SPANISH TRANSLATIONS AND EDITIONS:

Elementos del derecho natural. 2 vols. Traducido del Latín al francés por Barbeyrac, y al castellano por C. M. B. García Suelto. Edición hecha bajo la dirección de José Rene Masson. París, 1825.

Elementos del derecho natural. 1 vol. Nueve. ed. rev. y cor. Burdeos, P. Beaume, 1834.

Same. 2d ed. 1 vol. Madrid, Imprenta de Don N. Llorenci, 1837.

Same. 2 vols. José Rene Masson Ed. Paris, Lecointe y Lassere, 1838.

AMERICAN EDITIONS:

Principles of Natural and Politic Law. 2 vols. Boston, Joseph Bustead, 1792.

Same. 2 vols. Cambridge, Mass., W. Hilliard, 1807.

Same. 2 vols. Philadelphia, Carey, 1823.

Same. 2 vols. Philadelphia, Carey, 1830.

Same. 2 vols. Philadelphia, Carey, 1832.

Same. 2 vols. in 1. Columbus, Ohio, Riley, 1859.

Same. 2 vols. in 1. Albany, N. Y., W. C. Little, 1867.

BIBLIOGRAPHY

ADAMS, JAMES TRUSLOW. The Founding of New England. *Boston, The Atlantic Monthly Press, 1921.*

— Revolutionary New England, 1691–1776. *Boston, The Atlantic Monthly Press, 1923.*

ADAMS, JOHN. Works, 10 vols. Edited by C. F. Adams. *Boston, Little and Brown, 1851.*

ADAMS, R. G. Political Ideas of the American Revolution. *Durham, N. C., Trinity College Press, 1922.*

ALLEGHENY COLLEGE. Catalogus Bibliothicae Collegi Alleghenieensis. *Aprid Meadville, Thomae Atkinson et Soc., 1823.*

AMERICAN LITERARY, SCIENTIFIC, AND MILITARY ACADEMY. Catalogue of the Officers and Cadets. Norwich, Vermont. *Woodstock, Vt., David Watson, 1822.*

— Catalogue of the Officers and Cadets. Middletown, Connecticut. *Woodstock, Vt., David Watson, 1823.*

— Catalogue of the Officers and Cadets. Middletown, Connecticut. *Woodstock, Vt., David Watson, 1826.*

AMHERST COLLEGE. A Catalogue of the Library. *Amherst, W. Faxon, 1855.*

ARISTOTLE. Works, 10 vols. Edited by W. D. Ross and translated by B. Jowett. *Oxford, Clarendon Press, 1921.*

ARMORY, FRANCIS. Catalogue of Books to be Sold December 21, 1814. *Boston, John Eliot, 1814.*

— Catalogue of Books to be Sold December 20, 1815. *Boston, F. Armory, 1815.*

BALDWIN, ALICE M. The New England Clergy and the American Revolution. *Durham, N. C., Duke University Press, 1928.*

BALDWIN, SIMEON. An Oration in Commemoration of the Declaration of Independence and Establishment of the Constitution of the United States of America. *New Haven, J. Meigs, 1788.*

BALDWIN, S. E. The American Judiciary. *New York, The Century Company, 1925.*

— "The Study of Elementary Law." *Yale Law Journal, XIII (October, 1903), 1-15.*

BALTIMORE. A Catalogue of the Mercantile Library of Baltimore. *Baltimore, John W. Woods, 1851.*

BALTIMORE ATHENAEUM. A Catalogue of Books in the Library. *Baltimore, John O. Toy, 1927.*

BECKER, CARL. The Declaration of Independence. *New York, Harcourt, Brace and Company, 1922.*

BEDLINGTON AND EWER. A Catalogue of Books to be Sold in Boston. *Boston, S. Ethridge, 1822.*

BENNETT, EDMUND H. Syllabus of Law Studies Prepared for Harvard Law School Students. *n.d.*

BENOIST, CHARLES. "L'Influence des idées de Machiavel." Académie de Droit International, *Recueil des Cours,* 1925, Vol. IV (Whole No. 9, Paris, 1926).

BERNARD, EDWARD. An Election Sermon. *Boston, Richard Draper, 1766.*

BIBLIOGRAPHIE UNIVERSELLE. A. Thoisnier Desplaces, éditeur, *Paris, 1843.*

BLACKSTONE, WILLIAM. An Analysis of the Laws of England. 3d ed. *Oxford, Clarendon Press, 1758.*

— Commentaries on the Laws of England, 4 vols. 2d ed. *Oxford, Clarendon Press, 1766.*

BLAKE, D. T. A Discourse, Introductory to a Course of Law Lectures Delivered at Columbia College, 1810. *New York, Gould, Banks and Gould, 1810.*

BLAKE AND CUNNINGHAM. A Catalogue of Books, Including the Remains of the Library of the Late Reverend Mr. Cary. Sold at Auction, February 20, 1818. *Boston, Blake and Cunningham's Office, 1818.*

BLAND, RICHARD. An Inquiry Into the Rights of the British Colonies. Edited by E. G. Swem. *Richmond, Appeals Press, 1922.*

BOEGNER, MARC. "L'Influence de la reforme sur le development du droit international." Académie de Droit International, *Recueil des Cours*, 1925, Vol. I (Whole No. 6, Paris, 1926).

BORGEAUD, CHARLES. Histoire de l'université de Genève, 2 vols. *Genève, Georg and Company, 1900.*

— Pages d'histoire nationale. *Genève, Georg and Company, 1934.*

BOSTON ATHENAEUM. A Catalogue of Books. *Boston, W. L. Lewis, 1827.*

— A Catalogue of the Library, 1807–1871, 5 vols. *Boston, 1874.*

BOSTON LIBRARY. A Catalogue of Books. *Boston, John H. Eastburn, 1854.*

BOSTON PUBLIC LIBRARY. A Catalogue of Books. *Boston, J. Wilson and Son, 1854.*

BOWDOIN, JAMES. A Catalogue of Books left in the Possession of Major General Burgoyne. *Boston, September 9, 1775.*

BOWDOIN COLLEGE. A Catalogue of the Library. *Brunswick, John Griffin, 1821.*

— A Catalogue of the Officers and Students. *Brunswick, Joseph Griffin, 1826.*

BRIDGE, EBENEZER. An Election Sermon. *Boston, Green and Russell, 1767.*

BROADSIDES. A Catalogue of Books sold in the city of Vendue. *1769.*

BROWN UNIVERSITY. A Catalogue of the Library. Edited by C. C. Jewett. *Andover, Allen, Morrill and Wardell, 1843.*

— A Catalogue of the Library and Members of the United Brothers Society. *Providence, A. Crawford Greene, 1853. Instituted in 1806.*

— A Catalogue of the Officers and Students of Brown University. *Andover, Allen, Morrill, and Wardell, 1824.*

— Records of Brown University, 1824–1825.

BRUCE, PHILIP ALEXANDER. Institutional History of Virginia, 2 vols. *New York, G. P. Putnam's Sons, 1910.*

BUCKMINSTER, J. S. A Catalogue of the Library of. *Boston, John Eliot, 1812. Sold at auction.*

BURLAMAQUI, JEAN JACQUES. Principes du droit naturel, 1 vol. *Genève, Barrillot & fils, 1747.*

— Principes du droit naturel, 2 vols. in 1. *Genève, Barrillot & fils, 1747.*

— Principles of Natural Law, 1 vol. Translated by T. Nugent. *London, J. Nourse, 1752.*

— Principles of Politic Law: Being a sequel to the Principles of Natural Law. 1 vol. *London, J. Nourse, 1752.*

— Principles of Natural and Politic Law, 2 vols. *London, J. Nourse, 1752.*

— Principles of Natural and Politic Law, 2 vols. *London, C. Nourse, 1784.*

— Principles of Natural and Politic Law, 2 vols. *Columbus, Ohio, Riley, 1859.*

BUTTERWORTH, J. A Catalogue of Law Books. *London, Jacques and Company, 1801.*

CALHOUN, JOHN C. Works, 6 vols. Edited by R. K. Cralle, *New York, D. Appleton and Company, 1854–1856.*

CAREY, LEA AND BLANCHARD. A Catalogue of Books Sold by P. Thompson. *Washington, 1833.*

CARLISLE, PENNA. A Catalogue of Books Belonging to the Carlisle Library Company. *Carlisle, George Kline, 1797.*

CARLYLE, R. W. and A. J. A History of Mediaeval Political Theory in the West, 5 vols. *London, William Blackwood and Sons, 1928.*

CARPENTER, W. S. The Development of American Political Thought. *Princeton, Princeton University Press, 1930.*

Catalogue of All the Books Printed in the United States. *Boston, Published by the Booksellers of Boston, 1804.*

Catalogue of the Library of the Writers to His Majesty's Signet. *Edinburgh, The University Press, 1805.*

Catalogue des livres de droit et de jurisprudence. Ouvrages de fonds et en nombre. Auguste Durand, éditeur. *Paris, Libraire de la Bibliotheque, de la Court Imperiale et de L'Ordre des avocats, 1861.*

Catalogue of a Valuable Library of Books or Prints, Sold at Auction by Mr. James Christie. *London, 1797.*

CHAMPION, JUDAH. An Election Sermon. *Hartford, E. Watson, 1776.*

CHARLESTON, S. C. A Catalogue of Books Belonging to the Apprentice's Library Society. *Charleston, B. B. Hussy, 1840.*

CHARLESTON LIBRARY SOCIETY. Catalogue of Books. *London, W. Strahan, 1750.*

— Catalogue of Books. *Charleston, A. E. Miller, 1826. First complete catalogue.*

CHINARD, GILBERT. The Correspondence of Jefferson and Du Pont de Nemours. *Baltimore, The Johns Hopkins Press, 1931.*

— "Introduction to Pensées Choisies de Montesquieu tirées du 'Common-Place Book' de Thomas Jefferson." *Paris, Société d'édition "Les Belles Lettres," 1925.*

— Letters of Lafayette and Jefferson. *Baltimore, The Johns Hopkins Press, 1929.*

— Thomas Jefferson. *Boston, Little, Brown and Company, 1929.*

CHIPMAN, NATHANIEL. Principles of Government. *Burlington, Vt., Edward Smith, 1833.*

— Sketches of the Principles of Government. *Rutland, Vt., J. Lyon, 1793.*

CINCINNATI LAW LIBRARY ASSOCIATION. A Catalogue of Books Belonging to the Cincinnati Law Library Association. *1852.*

CLARK, JONAS. Election Sermon. *Boston, J. Gill and B. Edes and Sons, 1781.*

CLARKE, JOHN. Letters to a Student in the University of Cambridge, Massachusetts. *Boston, Samuel Hall, 1796.*

COKE, EDWARD. Institutes of the Laws of England or a Commentary upon Littleton, 2 vols. *Philadelphia, R. H. Small, 1853.*

COLBY, JAMES F. Legal and Political Studies in Dartmouth College, 1796–1896.

— "The Collegiate Study of Law." *American Bar Association Reports, XIX (1896), 521-41.*

CONWAY, M. D. The Life of Thomas Paine, 2 vols. *New York, G. P. Putnam's Sons, 1892.*

COOLEY, KEESE, AND HILL, Auctioneers. Catalogue of Valuable Collection of Books. *New York, 1848.*

COOPER, SAMUEL. The Crisis. *London, W. Griffin, 1766.*

— "Diary of Samuel Cooper, 1775–1776." *American Historical Review, VI (January, 1901), 310-41.*

— An Election Sermon. *Boston, T. and J. Fleet, and J. Gill, 1780.*

— "Letters of Samuel Cooper to Thomas Pownall, 1769–1777." *American Historical Review, VIII (January, 1903), 301-30.*

COOPER, THOMAS. Political Essays. 2d ed. *Philadelphia, Robert Campbell, 1800.*

CORWIN, EDWARD S. "The 'Higher Law' Background of American Constitutional Law." *Harvard Law Review, XLII (December, 1928), 149-85; (January, 1929), 365-409.*

COURT OF CHANCERY. Catalogue of the Library of the Court of Chancery. *April 1, 1843. Assembly No. 166. New York.*

CUSTIS, JOHN PARKER. Catalogue of Library of. *Tyler Magazine, Vol. IX. Inventory of 1782.*

DAIRE, M. E. Physiocrates. *Paris, Guillaumen, 1846.*

DANA, JAMES. An Election Sermon. *Hartford, Hudson and Goodwin, 1779.*

DARTMOUTH COLLEGE. A Catalogue of Books Belonging to the Social Friend's Library, October, 1931. *Hanover, Thomas Masson, 1831.*

— A Catalogue of the Officers and Students, October, 1822. *Concord, Statesman and Register Press, 1822.*

— A Catalogue of the Officers and Students, 1826. *Concord, Statesman and Register Press, 1826.*

— A Catalogue of the Officers and Students, 1827. *Concord, Statesman and Register Press, 1827.*

— A Catalogue of the Officers and Students, 1828. *Concord, Statesman and Register Press, 1828.*

DEPARTMENT OF STATE OF THE U. S. Catalogue of the Library of the Department of State of the United States. *May, 1830.*

DICKINSON, EDWIN D. "Changing Concepts and the Doctrine of Incorporation." *American Journal of International Law, XXVI (April, 1932), 239-60.*

DICKINSON, JOHN. Writings, 1 vol. Edited by P. L. Ford. *Brooklyn, Historical Printing Club, 1894.*

DIDIER, EUGENE. "Thomas Jefferson as a Lawyer." *The Green Bag, XV (April, 1903), 153-59.*

DOOR, EDWARD. An Election Sermon. *Hartford, Thomas Green, 1765.*

DUGUIT, LEON. Traite de droit constitutionnel, 5 vols. 3d ed. *Paris, E. de Boccard, 1927.*

DULANEY, DANIEL. Considerations on the Propriety of Imposing Taxes in the British Colonies for the Purpose of Raising a Revenue. *New York, John Holt, 1765.*

DUNNING, W. A. Political Theories from Luther to Montesquieu. *New York, The Macmillan Company, 1924.*

DUPIN, M. Manuel des étudians en droit des jeunes avocatis. Recueil d'opuscules de jurisprudence. *Paris, Joubert, Libraire-Éditeur, Rue de Gres, Pres L'École de droit, 1835.*

ELIOT, ANDREW. An Election Sermon. *Boston, Green and Russell, 1765.*

ELLIOT, JONATHAN. The Debates in the Several State Conventions and the Adoption of the Federal Constitution, 5 vols. *Philadelphia, J. B. Lippincott and Company, 1836.*

ERSKINE, JOHN. An Institute of the Law of Scotland, 2 vols. 5th ed. *Edinburgh, Bell and Bradute, 1812.*

EVANS, CHARLES. American Bibliography, 12 vols. *Chicago, Blakely Press, 1903-1904, 1907.*

FAIRLIE, JOHN A. "The Separation of Powers." *Michigan Law Review, XXI (February, 1923), 393-436.*

FALCONET, M. Catalogue de la bibliotheque de Few M. Falconet, Medecin Consultant du Roi, et Doyen des Medecins de la Faculté de Paris. *Paris, Chez Barrois, Libraire, 1763.*

FEDERALIST, THE. Edited by H. C. Lodge. *New York, G. P. Putnam's Sons, 1889.*

FERGUSON, ADAM. An Essay of the History of Civil Society. 5th ed. *London, T. Cadell, 1782.*

FISHER, SYDNEY GEORGE. The Struggle for American Independence, 2 vols. *Philadelphia, J. B. Lippincott Company, 1908.*

FORD, TIMOTHY. Americanus, The Constitutionalist or an Enquiry How Far it is Expedient and Proper to Alter the Constitution of South Carolina. *Charleston, Markland, M'Iver and Company, 1794.*

FOSTER, HERBERT D. Collected Papers of. *Privately printed,* *1929.*

FRANCK, ADOLPHIE. Réformateurs et publicistes de l'Europe; moyen age—renaissance. *Paris, Michel Lévy Frères, 1864.*

GERRY, ELBRIDGE. Observations on the New Constitution and on the Federal and State Conventions. *Boston, 1788.*

GOODRICH, DR. An Election Sermon. *Hartford, Hudson and Goodwin, 1787.*

GRANDE ENCYCLOPÉDIE, LA, 31 vols. *Paris, H. Lamirault et Cie., 1886–1902.*

GREEN, T. H. Principles of Political Obligation. *London, Longmans, Green and Company, 1924.*

GROTIUS, HUGO. De Jure Belli ac Pacis. Translated by W. Whewell. *Cambridge, 1853.*

— De Jure Belli ac Pacis Libri Tres, in quibus Jus Naturae & Gentium. *Washington, Carnegie Institution, 1913.*

GUERNSEY, R. S. Legal Bibliography. *New York, 1874.*

HAINES, CHARLES GROVE. The American Doctrine of Judicial Supremacy. *New York, The Macmillan Company, 1914.*

— The Revival of Natural Law Concepts. *Cambridge, Harvard University Press, 1930.*

HAMILTON, ALEXANDER. Works, 7 vols. Edited by J. C. Hamilton. *New York, John F. Trow, 1850–1851.*

— Works, 12 vols. Edited by H. C. Lodge. *New York, G. P. Putnam's Sons, 1904.*

HARRIS, THADDEUS M., Librarian of Harvard University. A Selected Catalogue of the Most Esteemed Publications in the English Language, Proper to form a Social Library with an Introduction upon the Choice of Books. *Boston, T. Thomas and E. J. Andrews, 1793.*

HARVARD UNIVERSITY. Catalogue of the Law Library. 2d ed. *Cambridge, E. W. Metcalf and Company, 1846.*

— Catalogue of the Library, 2 vols. *Cambridge, E. W. Metcalf and Company, 1830.*

— Catalogus Bibliotheca Harvardiania. *Boston, Thomae et Johannis Fleet, 1790.*

— Catalogus Librorum in Bibliotheca Cantabrigiensi, selectus, Frenquentiorem in usem Harvardinatum, qui gradu Baccalaurei in artuses. *Boston, Edes and Gill, 1773.*

— "Circulating Letter Relating to Harvard University." *North American Review, VI (March, 1818), 421-30.*

— The Laws of. *Boston, John and Thomas Fleet, 1798.*

HASTINGS, WILLIAM G. "Montesquieu and Anglo-American Institutions." *Illinois Law Review, XIII (Celebration Essays in Honor of John H. Wigmore, 1918), 419-30.*

HATBORO, PENNA. "A Colonial Reading List from the Union Library of Hatboro, Penna." Edited by Chester T. Hallenbeck. *Pennsylvania Magazine of History and Biography, LVI (October, 1932), No. 4.*

HATBOROUGH, UNION LIBRARY OF. A Catalogue of Books. 5th ed. *Philadelphia, T. E. Chapman, 1847.*

— A Catalogue of Books. 6th ed. *Morristown, National Defender Office, 1858.*

HAVEN, JASON. An Election Sermon. *Boston, Richard Draper, 1769.*

HAY, GEORGE. A Treatise on Expatriation. *Washington, A. & G. Way, 1814.*

HAZELTINE, H. D. "The Influence of Magna Carta on American Constitutional Development." *Columbia Law Review, XVII (January, 1917), 1-33.*

HITCHCOCK, GAD. An Election Sermon. *Boston, Edes and Gill, 1774.*

HOBBES, THOMAS. Leviathan. Everyman Edition. *New York, E. P. Dutton & Company, 1928.*

HOFFMAN, DAVID. An Address to Students of Law in the United States. *Baltimore, J. D. Toy, 1824. (Circular)*

— Course of Legal Study, 2 vols. 2d ed. *Baltimore, Joseph Neal, 1836.*

— A Course of Legal Study Respectfully Addressed to the Students of Law in the United States. *Baltimore, Coale and Maxwell, 1817.*

— Introductory Lecture and Syllabus of a Course of Lectures Delivered in the University of Maryland. *Baltimore, J. D. Toy, 1837.*

— Legal Outlines. Being the substances of a course of lectures now delivered in the University of Maryland, 3 vols. Vol. I. *Baltimore, E. J. Coale, 1829.*

— Syllabus of a Course of Lectures on Law Proposed to be Delivered in the University of Maryland. *Baltimore, J. D. Toy, 1821.*

HOLDSWORTH, W. S. Some Lessons from our Legal History. *New York, The Macmillan Company, 1928.*

HOLMES, ABEL. The Life of Ezra Stiles. *Boston, Thomas and Andrews, 1798.*

HOLST, HERMANN EDUARD VON. The Constitutional and Political History of the United States, 8 vols. *Chicago, Callaghan and Company, 1876–1892.*

HONEYWELL, ROY J. "Nathaniel Chipman." *The New England Quarterly, V (July, 1932), 555-84.*

HOSMER, JAMES K. The Life of Thomas Hutchinson. *Boston, Houghton, Mifflin and Company, 1896.*

HOWARD, SIMEON. An Election Sermon. *Boston, John Gill, 1780.*

HUBNER, MARTIN. Essai sur l'histoire de droit naturel, 2 vols. *London, 1757.*

HUTCHINSON, THOMAS. Speeches of Thomas Hutchinson to the General Assembly, 1773. *Boston, Edes and Gill, 1773.*

INNER TEMPLE. Catalogue of the Library of. *London, T. C. Hansard, 1833.*

IREDELL, JAMES. Life and Correspondence of James Iredell, 2 vols. Edited by Griffith J. McRee. *New York, D. Appleton and Company, 1857.*

JANET, PAUL. Histoire de la science politique. *Paris, Librairie philosophique de Ladrange, 1872.*

JAY, JOHN. The Correspondence and Public Papers of John Jay, 2 vols. Edited by H. P. Johnston. *New York, G. P. Putnam's Sons, 1890.*

JEFFERSON, THOMAS. The Commonplace Book. Edited by Gilbert Chinard. Johns Hopkins Studies in Romance Literature and Languages, II. *Baltimore, The Johns Hopkins Press, 1926.*

— Writings, 20 vols. Memorial Edition. *Washington, 1907.*

JOHNSON, SAMUEL. A Catalogue of Books Read by. Edited by H. and C. Schneider. *New York, Columbia University Press, 1929.*

JOHNSON, STEPHEN. Election Sermon. *New London, T. Green, 1770.*

JONES, HOWARD MUMFORD. America and French Culture, 1750–1848. *Chapel Hill, The University of North Carolina Press, 1927.*

KENT, JAMES. Commentaries on American Law, 4 vols. Edited by C. M. Barnes. *Boston, Little, Brown and Company, 1884.*

— Dissertations being the Preliminary Part of a Course of Law Lectures. *New York, George Foreman, 1795.*

— An Introductory Lecture to a Course of Law Lectures delivered November 17, 1794. *New York, Francis Childs, 1794.*

KILBOURN, DWIGHT C. The Bench and Bar of Litchfield County, Connecticut, 1709–1909. *Litchfield, Kilbourn, 1909.*

KLUBER, J. L. Droit des gens. 2d ed. *Paris, Guillaumin et Cie., 1874.*

KNAPP, SAMUEL L. Biographical Sketches of Eminent Lawyers, Statesmen and Men of Letters. *Boston, Richardson and Lord, 1821.*

LAW BOOKSELLERS ASSOCIATION. A Catalogue of Law Books, Ancient and Modern. *London, W. Pople, 1823.*

LEAVITT, LORD AND COMPANY. Catalogue of Books for Sale. Compiled by George P. Putnam. *New York, 1836.*

LEXINGTON, KY., LIBRARY COMPANY. A Catalogue of Books. *Lexington, Thomas Smith, 1821.*

LIBRARY OF CONGRESS. Catalogue of the Library of Congress. *Washington, Jonathan Elliot, 1815.*

LIDDLE, W. F. Different Libraries in Rochester, New York, August 31, 1847. *Rochester, Shepard and Read, 1847.*

LOCKE, JOHN. Of Civil Government. Everyman Edition. *New York, E. P. Dutton and Company, 1924.*

LOCKWOOD, SAMUEL. An Election Sermon. *New London, Thomas Green, 1774.*

LOVEJOY, A. O. "The Supposed Primitivism of Rousseau's Discourse on Inequality." *Modern Philology, XXI (November, 1923), 165-86.*

McILWAIN, CHARLES HOWARD. The American Revolution: A Constitutional Interpretation. *New York, The Macmillan Company, 1924.*

MACKAY, R. A. "Coke—Parliamentary Sovereignty or the Supremacy of the Law?" *Michigan Law Review, XXII (January, 1924), 215-47.*

M'KEAN, JOSEPH. Catalogue of the Select Library of the Late Reverend J. M'Kean. *Boston, John Eliot, 1816.*

McLAUGHLIN, ANDREW C. Confederation and the Constitution, 1783–1789. *New York, Harpers, 1905.*

— The Courts, the Constitution and Parties; Studies in Constitutional History and Politics. *Chicago, University of Chicago Press, 1912.*

— The Foundations of American Constitutionalism. *New York, New York University Press, 1932.*

MADISON, JAMES. Letters and Writings, 4 vols. Edited by W. C. Rives. *Philadelphia, J. B. Lippincott and Company, 1865.*

MAINE. A Catalogue of Books in the State Library. *Augusta, Me., W. R. Smith and Company, 1843.*

MAINE, SIR HENRY J. S. Ancient Law. *New York, C. Scribner, 1864.*

MARCAGGI, V. Les origines de la déclaration des droits de l'homme de 1789. 2d ed. *Paris, Fontenoing, 1912.*

MARTENS, GEORG FRIEDRICH. A Summary of the Law of Nations, founded on the treatises and customs of the modern nations of Europe. Translated by William Cobbett. *Philadelphia, Thomas Bradford, 1795.*

MARTIN, CHARLES E. An Introduction to the Study of the American Constitution. *New York, Oxford University Press, 1926.*

MARVIN, J. G. Legal Bibliography of American, English, Irish, and Scotch Law Books. *Philadelphia, T. and T. W. Johnson, 1847.*

MASSACHUSETTS. Catalogue of the Library of the General Court of. *Boston, Dutton and Wentworth, 1831.*

Massachusetts Historical Society Proceedings, XVI (2d series), 1902.

MAYHEW, JONATHAN. Discourse Concerning Unlimited Submission and Non-Resistance to the Higher Powers; with Some Reflections on the Resistance made to King Charles I. . . . Boston, D. Fowle, 1750. Boston, Reprinted by Hall & Goss, 1818.

MEIGS, W. M. "Relation of the Judiciary to the Constitution." American Law Review, XIX (March-April, 1885), 175-203.

MONTESQUIEU, M. DE. Complete Works, 4 vols. London, T. Evans and W. Davis, 1777.

MORISON, SAMUEL ELLIOT. The Life and Letters of Harrison Gray Otis, 2 vols. Boston, Houghton Mifflin Company, 1913.

— ed. Sources and Documents Illustrating the American Revolution 1764–1788. Oxford, Clarendon Press, 1923.

MÜLLER, JOSEPH. "Oeuvre de toutes les confessions chrétiennes (églises) pour la paix internationale. Académie de Droit International, Recueil des Cours, 1930, Vol. I (Whole No. 31, Paris, 1931).

MULLETT, CHARLES F. "Coke and the American Revolution." Economica, XII (September, 1932), 457-71.

— Fundamental Law and the American Revolution. New York, Columbia University Press, 1933.

— "Some Political Writings of James Otis." University of Missouri Studies, IV (July, 1929), 257-357; (October 1929), 369-432.

NEVINS, ALLAN. The American States During and After the Revolution, 1775–1789. New York, The Macmillan Company, 1927.

NEW YORK CITY. Catalogue of the Books in the Mercantile Library of the City of New York. New York, F. F. Taylor, 1866.

NEW YORK SOCIETY LIBRARY. The Charter, By-Laws and Names of the Members, With a Catalogue of the Books Belonging to the Library. New York, Hugh Gaine, 1789.

— Same. New York, Hugh Gaine, 1773.

— Same. New York, T. J. Swords, 1793.

— Same. New York, T. J. Swords, 1800.

— Same. New York, James van Worden, 1838.

Nys, Ernest. Les États-Unis et le droit des gens. *Bruxelles, Bureau de la Revue, 1909*.

— Études de droit international et le droit politique, 2 vols. *Paris, A. Fontenoing, 1896*.

Paine, Thomas. The Rights of Man. *London, J. Jordan, 1791*.

Parrington, Vernon Louis. Main Currents in American Thought, 3 vols. Vol. I. The Colonial Mind, 1620–1800; Vol. II. The Romantic Revolution in America, 1800–1860; Vol. III. The Beginnings of Critical Realism in America, 1860–1920. *New York, Harcourt, Brace and Company, 1927–1930*.

Parsons, Theophilus. A Catalogue of the Library of. Sold at Auction March 1, 1814, at Francis Armory's Store. *Boston, Francis Armory, 1814*.

— Memoirs of Theophilus Parsons. Edited by Theophilus Parsons, Jr. *Boston, Ticknor and Fields, 1859*.

Pason, Phillips. An Election Sermon. *Boston, John Gill, 1778*.

Philadelphia. Catalogue of Books Belonging to the Library Association of. *Philadelphia, William Bradford, 1765*.

— A Catalogue of a Scarce and Valuable Collection of Books at the American Circulating Library of. Edited by William Prichard. *Philadelphia, 1785*.

— A Catalogue of Books of the Library Company of. *Philadelphia, Zachariah Poulson, 1789*.

— Same. *Philadelphia, C. Sherman and Company, 1835*.

Philadelphia Bar Association. Catalogue of Library of. *Philadelphia, James Humphrey, 1805*.

Piedelievre, R. Precis de droit international public ou droit des gens. *Paris, E. Pichon, 1894*.

Plato. The Republic. Translated by B. Jowett. *New York, Willey Book Company, 1901*.

Pollock, Sir Frederick. "The History of the Law of Nature." *Columbia Law Review, I (January, 1901), 11-32*.

Poore, Benjamin P. The Federal and State Constitutions, Colonial Charters, and other Organic Laws of the United States, 2 vols. *Washington, Government Printing Office, 1878*.

POUND, ROSCOE. "Grotius in the Science of Law." *American Journal of International Law, XIX (October, 1925), 685-88.*

— "The Theory of Judicial Decision." *Harvard Law Review, XXXVI (April, 1923), 641-62; (May, 1923), 802-25; (July, 1923), 940-59.*

PRIESTMAN'S LIBRARY. A Catalogue of Books. M. Thomas, Auctioneer. *Philadelphia, 1831.*

PROVIDENCE ATHENAEUM. Catalogue of the Library. *Providence, Wm. Marshall and Company, 1833.*

PUFENDORF, SAMUEL. De Officio Hominis et Civis juxta Legem Maturalem libri duo. Translated by H. F. Wright. *New York, Oxford University Press, 1927.*

— Of the Law of Nature and Nations. Translated by Basil Kennett. *Oxford, 1710.*

QUEEN'S COLLEGE, CAMBRIDGE UNIVERSITY. A Catalogue of the Library of the College of St. Margaret and St. Bernard, 2 vols. *London, S. and R. Bentley, 1827.*

Records of the Federal Convention of 1787, The. 3 vols. Edited by Max Farrand. *New Haven, Yale University Press, 1911.*

REED, A. Z. Training for the Public Profession of Law. Carnegie Foundation for the Advancement of Teaching, Bulletin No. 15. *New York, 1921.*

REEVES, J. S. "La Communaute Internationale." Académie de Droit International, *Recueil des Cours*, 1924, Vol. II (Whole No. 3, Paris, 1925).

— "Influence of Law of Nature upon International Law in the United States." *American Journal of International Law, III (July, 1909), 547-61.*

RHODE ISLAND COLLEGE. A Catalogue of Books Belonging to the Library. *Providence, J. Carter, 1793.*

— A Catalogue of Books ordered from England. *1783.*

RITCHIE, DAVID G. Natural Rights. *London, George Allen, 1894.*

ROUSSEAU, JEAN JACQUES. The Social Contract. Everyman Edition. *New York, E. P. Dutton and Company, 1923.*

RUTHERFORTH, THOMAS. Institutes of Natural Law, 2 vols. *Cambridge, J. Bentham, 1754.*

SABIN, JOSEPH. Bibliothea Americana. A Dictionary of Books Relating to America from its Discovery to the Present Time. *New York, 1868–1892.*

SALMOND, JOHN W. "The Law of Nature." *Law Quarterly Review, XI (April, 1895), 121-43.*

SCOTT, JAMES BROWN. "John Jay, First Chief Justice of the United States." *Columbia Law Review, VI (May, 1906), 289-325.*

SHUTE, DANIEL. An Election Sermon. *Boston, Richard Draper, 1768.*

SMITH, J. ALLEN. The Growth and Decadence of Constitutional Government. *New York, Henry Holt and Company, 1930.*

SMITH, JOHN AUGUSTINE. A Syllabus of the Lectures Delivered to the Senior Students in the College of William and Mary on Government. *Philadelphia, W. Fry, 1817.*

SOUTH CAROLINA COLLEGE. A Catalogue of Books Belonging to the Library, August 23, 1814. *Columbia, D. and J. J. Faust, 1814.*

SPILSBURG, WILLIAM HOLDEN. Lincoln's Inn: Its Ancient and Modern Buildings, with an Account of the Library. *London, William Pickering, 1850.*

SPRAGUE, WILLIAM B. Annals of the American Pulpit, 4 vols. *New York, Robert Carter and Brothers, 1858.*

STEINER, B. R. "Law Libraries in Colonial Virginia." *The Green Bag (August, 1897), 351-54.*

STEVENS, BENJAMIN. An Election Sermon. *Boston, John Draper, 1761.*

STILES, EZRA. Literary Diary, 3 vols. Edited by F. B. Dexter. *New York, C. Scribner's Sons, 1901.*

STILLÉ, CHARLES J. The Life and Times of John Dickinson, 1732–1808. *Philadelphia, J. B. Lippincott Company, 1891.*

STILLMAN, SAMUEL. Good News from a Far Country. *Boston, Kneeland and Adams, 1766.*

STORY, JOSEPH. Commentaries on the Constitution of the United States, 2 vols. 5th ed. Edited by Nelville M. Bigelow. *Boston, Little, Brown and Company, 1891.*

—— "Review of David Hoffman's A Course of Legal Study Respectfully Addressed to the Students of Law in the United States. Coale and Maxwell. Baltimore. 1817." *North American Review, VI (November, 1817), 45.*

TEMPLETON, GEORGE. A Catalogue of Congressional Documents and of Scarce Books for Sale, Washington, 1833. *Washington, Globe Office, 1833.*

THACH, CHARLES C. The Creation of the Presidency, 1775–1789. *Baltimore, The Johns Hopkins University Press, 1922.*

THAYER, JAMES BRADLEY. John Marshall. *Boston, Houghton Mifflin Company, 1901.*

— "The Teaching of English Law at Universities." *Harvard Law Review, IX (October, 1895), 169-84.*

THEOLOGICAL SEMINARY. A Catalogue of the Library, Andover, Massachusetts. Edited by Oliver A. Taylor. *Andover, Gould and Newman, 1838.*

THORNTON, JOHN WINGATE. The Pulpit of the American Revolution. *Boston, Gould and Lincoln, 1860.*

THORPE, F. N. The Federal and State Constitutions, Colonial Charters, and other Organic Laws of the States, 7 vols. *Washington, Government Printing Office, 1906.*

TUCKER, JOHN. An Election Sermon. *Boston, Richard Draper, 1771.*

TUCKER, JOHN RANDOLPH. The Constitution of the United States, 2 vols. Edited by Henry St. George Tucker. *Chicago, Callaghan and Company, 1899.*

TUCKER, JOSIAH. The Notions of Mr. Locke, and His Followers, that all Civil Governments whatever, not founded on the personal choice of the governed, are so many usurpations on the unalienable rights of Mankind. *Gloucester, 1778.*

— A Treatise Concerning Civil Government. *London, Cadell, 1781.*

TURNER, CHARLES. An Election Sermon. *Boston, Richard Draper, 1775.*

TYLER, LYON G. Early Courses and Professors at William and Mary College. *Williamsburg, Va., 1904.*

— "A Few Facts from the Records of William and Mary College." *American Historical Association Papers, IV (October, 1890), 453-67.*

TYLER, M. C. Literary History of the American Revolution. *New York, G. P. Putnam's Sons, 1876.*

VATTEL, EMERICH. Law of Nations. *Philadelphia, T. and J. W. Johnson, 1844.*

VIRGINIA. A Catalogue of the Library of the University of Virginia. *Charlottesville, Gilmer, Davis and Company, 1828.*

— Same. *Richmond, Samuel Shepherd and Company, 1829.*

VOORHIES, HON. S. A. A Catalogue of Law Books for Sale. *New York, William Osborn, 1844.*

WARREN, CHARLES. History of the American Bar. *Boston, Little, Brown and Company, 1911.*

— History of the Harvard Law School, 3 vols. *New York, Lewis Publishing Company, 1908.*

WASHINGTON, D. C. A Catalogue of Books Belonging to the Library of. *Washington, Gale and Seaton, 1835. Inventory of 1834.*

WEEKS, STEPHEN B. "Libraries and Literature in North Carolina in the Eighteenth Century." *Annual Report of the American Historical Association, 1895, pp. 171-267.*

WEISS, A. "États Étrangers Devant Les Tribunaux." Académie de Droit International, *Recueil des Cours,* 1923, Vol. I (Whole No. 1, Paris, 1925).

WELLS, WILLIAM V. The Life and Public Services of Samuel Adams. *Boston, Little, Brown and Company, 1865.*

WEST, JOHN, Bookseller. A Catalogue of Books Printed and Published in America for Sale at the Bookstore of. *Boston, 1799.*

WEST, SAMUEL. An Election Sermon. *Boston, John Gill, 1776.*

WHITEHALL, BOND AND CO., Auctioneers. Catalogue of a Collection of Valuable Books to be Sold, Boston, 1837. *Boston, John H. Eastburn, 1837.*

WILDE, NORMAN. The Ethical Basis of the State. *Princeton, Princeton University Press, 1924.*

WILLIAMS, ABRAHAM. An Election Sermon. *Boston, S. Kneeland, 1762.*

WILLOUGHBY, WESTEL W. The Ethical Basis of Political Authority. *New York, The Macmillan Company, 1930.*

WILSON, JAMES. Works, 3 vols. Edited by Bird Wilson. *Philadelphia, Lorenzo Press, 1804.*

— Works, 2 vols. Edited by James DeWitt Andrews. *Chicago, Callaghan and Company, 1892.*

WILTSE, CHARLES M. The Jeffersonian Tradition in American Democracy. *Chapel Hill, The University of North Carolina Press, 1935.*

WIRT, WILLIAM. A Catalogue of Law Library of.

WITHERSPOON, JOHN. Lectures on Moral Philosophy. Edited by V. L. Collins. *Princeton, Princeton University Press, 1912.*

WRIGHT, BENJAMIN FLETCHER, JR. American Interpretations of Natural Law. *Cambridge, Harvard University Press, 1931.*

— "The Origin of Separation of Powers in America." *Economica, XIII (May, 1933), 169-85.*

WRIGHT, THOMAS GODDARD. Literary Culture in Early New England, 1620–1730. Edited by his wife. *New Haven, Yale University Press, 1920.*

YALE, GREGORY. Catalogue of the Law Library of Gregory Yale, 1849. Jacksonville, East Florida. *Savannah, Ga., Edward C. Councell, 1849.*

YALE COLLEGE. Catalogue of Books belonging to the Calliopean Society. *Yale College, June, 1831.*

— Catalogue of Books in the Linonian Brothers and Moral Libraries. *New Haven.*

YALE LAW SCHOOL, MEMBERS OF. Two Centuries' Growth of American Law, 1701–1901. *New York, Charles Scribner's Sons, 1901.*

YALE UNIVERSITY. A Catalogue of the Library. *Printed at the Journal Office, 1823.*

INDEX

A

Adams, John, paraphrased Burlamaqui, 75; read Burlamaqui, 90; relied on Burlamaqui, 117-19; on right of revolution, 127; on consent theory, 134-35; on the constitution, 146-47; on separation of powers, 157-58

American Circulating Library of Philadelphia, 83

American Literary, Scientific and Military Academy, The, 102

Aristotle, 3, 10, 12, 131

B

Barbeyrac, 35

Becker, Carl, 120

Bernard, Edward, 157

Blackstone, William, 82; first American edition, 104; relation to the Declaration of Independence, 124; definition of constitution, 154

Bliss, George, 86

Booksellers, 95

Borgeaud, Charles, 14

Bowdoin College, 101

Bowdoin, James, 90

Brown University, 83, 94, 95, 101

Burlamaqui, Jean Jacques, biography of, 185-87; bibliography of, 188-92; acceptance of the Aristotelian thesis, 10-11; on social nature of man, 11-12, 15; on natural liberty, 13, 15; on natural society, 14; on happiness, 16-18; origin of state,

24-28; natural law, 18-20; social compact, 28, 30; on sovereignty, 33-36; popular sovereignty, 36-37; on limited and absolute sovereignty, 38-39, 40; on nature of law, 43-44; the characteristics of law, 45-47; on fundamental law, 52-55, 72, 167; on the higher law, 53-54; on the nature of the constitution, 56-57, 167; on separation of powers, 62-64, 66-67; on checks and balances, 67-68; on limited state, 71-73; on judicial review, 68-69, 71, 73-76; limited legislature, 72; works in libraries, 81-95; used as textbook in colleges, 95-102; American editions, 103-5; influence upon Declaration of Independence, 120-24; on popular sovereignty in America, 130-35; on natural law in colonies, 135-40; Tom Paine's similarity to, 123; relation to Jefferson, 122-23, 148, 150, 159, 169; influence on: James Wilson, 124, 128, 132-34, 139, 145, 161, 172-75; John Adams, 127, 134, 146, 157-58; James Madison, 128, 139, 151, 164, 173-74; the clergymen, 131, 158; James Otis, 132, 138, 171; Alexander Hamilton, 116-17, 135, 161-63, 170, 172; concept of higher law, 136-39; written constitution, 143-54; Justice Story, 153-54; coördinate departments, 154-59; checks and balances, 159, 165; judicial review, 167

215

C

Calhoun, John C., 91
Carlyle, A. J., 10
Carlyle, R. W., 10
Charleston Library Society, 83
Chauncy, Roger, 89, 95
Checks and balances, 67-68, 75, 154-65
Chinard, Gilbert, 120-21, 149
Chipman, Nathaniel, 130
Clark, Jonas, 157
Clarke, John, 88, 98, 157
Coke, Sir Edward, 49-50, 70-71, 142
Colby, James F., 100
Columbia University, 84, 94, 96
Conservative revolt 1788, 124-27
Convention theory of state, 4, 6-7, 9, 11, 13, 14
Cooper, Samuel, 88, 110, 144, 158
Cooper, Thomas, 91
Corwin, E. S., 124, 137
Custis, John Parker, 89

D

Dartmouth College, 83, 94, 95, 100
Déclaration des droits de l'homme et du citoyen, 121
Declaration of Independence, 119, 121, 135
Dickinson, E. D., 20
Door, Edward, 137
Duguit, Leon, 32

E

Eliot, Andrew, quotes Burlamaqui, 87; on inalienable right of happiness, 110; on consent theory, 131; on limited government, 144
Essex Result, 152

F

Foster, H. D., 51
Fundamental law, Coke's concept of, 48-50; Locke's notion of, 51-52; Burlamaqui's idea of, 53-57; Burlamaqui and the American principle of, 143-54

G

Green, T. H., 7
Grotius, Hugo, 19, 80, 136

H

Haines, C. G., 169
Hamilton, Alexander, on natural rights, 116-17; on checks and balances, 161-62; on judicial review, 170, 172
Harris, Thaddeus M., 82
Harvard University, 86, 94, 95, 97-99
Higher Law, 48; Coke on, 49; Burlamaqui's concept of, 54; American interpretation of, 135-39
Hobbes, Thomas, on the state of nature, 5; on social contract, 6; on nature of the state, 21-22; binding force of law, 40-42
Hoffman, David, 98, 102-3
Hollis, Thomas, 82, 86, 97

I

Iredell, James, 153, 171

J

Jefferson, Thomas, the Declaration of Independence, 119-22; on fundamental law, 148-50; on coördinate departments, 159-61; on limited legislature, 169
Judicial review, 73-76, 166-75

K

Kames, Lord, 121, 123
Kent, James, 100, 129
Kirby, Ephraim, 89

L

Law of nature, Hobbes on, 5; Locke on, 8-10; Burlamaqui on, 16-17; as a higher law, 55; limiting nature of, 71-72, 135-40
Library Company of Philadelphia, 81